The Imposters

"*The Imposters* is a dynamic memoir, a rarity. Delicious, suspenseful and a great read. I looked forward to every chapter."

Alphie McCourt, author of *A Long Stone's Throw*

"This is an adventure in many ways, a story that moves fast and unpredictably, told with artistry, keen observation and zero affectation."

Peter Birkenhead, author of *Gonville*

"Marta Szabo writes beautifully — with a sharp eye for detail and nuance of feeling."

Melissa Coleman, author of *This Life Is in Your Hands*

The Guru Looked Good

"This is the story of a spiritual quest that begins in fervent trust and hope, and ultimately leads to hard-earned, clear-eyed wisdom. Marta Szabo's searching honesty and soaring spirit come flying off every page."

Daniel Shaw, LCSW, author of *Traumatic Abuse in Cults*

"Marta Szabo captures in this vibrant memoir a core experience of yearning that lives in many of us who seek inner peace and a life of fulfillment in the service of others. By courageously depicting her own story, Marta reveals how religion or any ideological path can turn from inspiring to stifling.

DeAnn Daigle, author of *Come So Far*

The First Two
Real Life Writing

Waiting, *etching by Richard Pantell*

The First Two

Real Life Writing

Marta Szabo

    108 Tinker Street
    Woodstock NY 12498
Ordering Information:
    For details, contact: MartaSzabo@AuthenticWriting.com
Print ISBN: 978-0-99-641221-6
eBook ISBN: 9780996412223
Printed in the United States of America
    First Edition
Design, production, editing, and illustration credits:
    Book design and production: small packages, inc
        smallpackages.com
    Cover Image: Rick Pantell
    Author Photo: Franco Vogt

for Fred
who made all the difference

CONTENTS

ACKNOWLEDGEMENTS

This book needs to include a few more names before it can get started. Special thanks to my dear friend, Val Vadeboncoeur, who bravely reviewed this manuscript as it prepared to begin its life as a public document. His editorial expertise, good humor and conscientious attention were all deeply appreciated.

Thank you to dear friend Rick Pantell for giving me permission to use his beautiful artwork on the cover. Rick is a leading artist of his time and can often be found teaching at the Art Students League in New York City.

I thank my two sisters, A and K. I am grateful to be part of our amazing threesome.

And lastly, I thank all my Authentic Writing companions. Together, we create the Authentic Writing workshops where I do almost all my writing. Every book I have written, including this one, was written there.

With Special Thanks

One of my very favorite films of all time is the documentary Man on Wire, depicting the hair-raising story of Philippe Petit stringing a cable between the twin towers of the World Trade Center in 1974 and walking back and forth, suspended over 1,000 feet above the city without a net. He held a long flexible pole in his hands. Except for that pole, he was as vulnerable as a leaf.

Setting off to create this book felt very much like being on that wire. So easy to fall off. I needed a long flexible pole. Luckily, I had one. Her name is Suzanne Bachner. Without her, the wind would have blown me off course and this book and I would not have crossed the abyss.

Suzanne Bachner, Artistic Director of JMTC Theatre, has been a successful playwright and director for decades. She is known for her dynamic, imaginative, witty productions and for nurturing the creative work of others. Not only is she an accomplished professional, she has a heart of gold.

Thank you, Suzanne, for being godmother to this project.

AT FIRST

I WANT TO WRITE ABOUT EVERYTHING AT ONCE, tell every story and show every scene from start to finish and the way they overlap, but it just can't be done. I can only show you one at a time, and never all of them.

I can tell you about Bird's and my walk just before dinner, along a ridge, the road cutting into a steep slope that fell below us on which tall trees grew and I wondered about their root systems, supporting their tall thick trunks on such steepness.

And I can tell you how usually now when I walk with Bird, the Golden Hound, I feel in the company of a friend, not a stranger like it was in the beginning when we did not speak each other's language, how sad and desperate that was for both of us, how now we walk and pause and respond to each other, almost always connected except perhaps when, nearing the end of a walk and Bird over-lingers, her nose deep under some bush, I get impatient.

But for this walk today I must tell you how we turned into the long-grass field and Bird began her running-circling-leaping dance of excitement, and I drank it in, delighting in her exuberance in the tall grass with still here and there those tiny flowers from summertime, buried in the grass like improbable pink stars.

And most of all I have to tell you about the sudden storm of wind that arose out of nowhere, bending branches, cascading leaves. The wind roared as if we were at sea. Bird picked up her pace, looking around her as she trotted, almost scared but not quite. I glimpsed the black form of a bird gliding through upper branches, half invisible, slipping from shadow to shadow. I kept my eye fixed on where the bird had landed, hoping that as we approached I would get a closer look and be able to identify it. I was not sure I'd be able to find it. Maybe, I thought, I had made a mistake and there was no bird, just a trick of shadows — but no, there it went. I couldn't name it until further out against the sky it spread its wings and coasted — turkey buzzard.

The storm of wind continued and I didn't want those moments to end, leaves raining down in colors, the crashing music of the wind.

PART ONE

THERE WAS A TIME

THERE WAS A TIME WHEN THE BEST THING was to sit on my father's lap in the morning and stir his coffee. We sat at the table in the room that didn't have a window, my mother on the other side of a counter where the refrigerator was, in the background, in the shadow.

From my father's lap I could see into the next room — big windows there and long filmy curtains billowing with brightness.

I don't know what's on the other side of those windows. But it's where my father goes after the coffee. Somehow, he gets out there, beyond the bright windows. I know that, once outside, he has to go downward, as if down a steep slope. These rooms we live in are perched above the place where he goes, and where he goes has to do with a train. He takes a thin hard brown suitcase that opens with bright hard clicks. Inside are only papers.

On the days when he does not go away, he puts me on his shoulders and we walk outside. He holds my ankles. "Don't pull my hair!" he laughs in protest. I hear the words, but they rush past me as if meant for someone else. Because I am not pulling his hair. I am holding on.

FATHER SWIMS

WHEN I WAS LITTLE and we went to the beach my father always left us. He set aside the Sunday New York Times to walk through the crowd down to the water, hitching up the navy blue knitted swimming trunks my mother had made him before I was born. Slowly he waded through the shallows, through the people jumping and doing normal things, until he was swimming past every single person, out to the horizon in a straight line further and further and further, his head never below water, just a black dot, until he was gone. And then later, he comes back out of nowhere, reaching for a towel, water streaming down his body, a laugh of pleasure on his face. And I wonder where he has been.

FATHER AND MOTHER

MY FATHER, THE HANDSOME HUNGARIAN. My mother, the sub-
dued Canadian.

The living room is full of my father's friends. Both of my parents call
them friends, but the guests are Hungarians. They are here because of my
father. The men wear suits, white shirts and ties. The women wear skirts
and jewelry. Everyone is old and they say "the war" a lot. Before the war.
After the war. That was during the war.

My father is at the center. The women look at him with glasses in their
hands. Everyone has a glass in their hands. He makes them laugh.

Mostly though the Hungarians are sad. You can tell.

My mother sits on the arm of the couch, not quite part of it, even when
they speak in accented English to include her. If she speaks, she sounds like
an outsider, her words like wooden blocks instead of the smooth pebbles of
party talk.

I sit on a chair and look at how my legs stick straight out. They do not
bend over the edge of the chair the way grown-up legs do. I like especially
the way ladies cross their legs. I wish mine were long enough to go over the
edge of the chair and then cross. I cross them anyway.

My father doesn't like my mother. He likes the other women who can
laugh and talk at the same time. Like the lady he waltzed down to the bottom of the driveway. I didn't see it, but he told me about it in the morning
so that I knew it was special and something no one else would do.

Everyone watches as my mother walks up the stairs. We can see her go
up through the railings. The top of her body disappears first and then all we
can see are her bare legs.

"Joan's legs are so scratched!" say the people.

It's because she likes to be outside. She grows strawberries and shows them to me, saying the word "strawberries" with excitement, as if we have stumbled upon buried treasure. She sells clumps of myrtle held in her hand, wrapped in newspaper, to people who drive up. She points out the kitchen window in the morning and says, "Look! A cardinal!"

I don't think anyone else here does the things my mother does. They are indoor people. Even when she puts on stockings and heels and a necklace and earrings, she is not like the other women who wear these things naturally.

I wish my mother would change. Can't she see that she needs to be different, that my father would like her better if she were different? Doesn't she know? If she knew she would change.

I want a different mother, one my father likes. In the meantime, he has me.

BUBBLEGUM PEOPLE

MY FATHER CLAIMED ME right away. I was his.

My little sister was my mother's.

"She looks just like you," said the grown-ups to my father. "And the baby looks like your wife." I did not know what they meant. I did not look like my father. My sister did not look like my mother. How could they say we looked like grown-ups? But it was unanimous, repeated over and over. I was my father's. She was my mother's.

I was glad to be on the winning team. I looked up into the bright sun of my father's attention and smiled back, flung my arms open and knew he knew everything.

"Do not be a bubblegum person," he warned me with a serious face and raised index finger. "Do not ever become a bubblegum person," and I knew what he meant.

Not all Americans were bubblegum people but all bubblegum people were American. They chewed gum. They watched TV during the daytime. The men wore tee shirts or plaid sport jackets. Their kids had runny noses and ate cereal. Their wives had dyed hair in rollers, long painted nails and drove station wagons.

My father laid out the correct choices clearly: classical music, literature, good theater, good opera, Europe, Hungary, villas, people with titles, good table manners, restaurants where they treat you with deference. I knew that some things were right and some things were not to even be tried because they were for bubblegum people only.

NO ONE ELSE

HIS SQUARE GOLD CUFFLINKS. His custom suits. Not many, but custom, made by the same tailor used by Katherine Hepburn, he said. He'd seen her there once. During some rich years.

The way he laced his leather shoes, not criss-crossing like everyone else, but lacing them so that they marched up the tongue in horizontal bars. The thick gold wedding band and thin gold lozenge of a Swiss watch on a leather strap.

Perhaps most of all the three black Mont Blanc pens, his as if no one else in the world had one, each identified by a fat white star at the tip. The ballpoint that opened with a lever. The pencil that swiveled open. But most especially, the thick fountain pen filled from a bottle of dark blue Quink ink sitting on his desk. His handwriting never casual, always a considered movement as if he were leaving a trace of himself for others to admire, the handwriting mysterious to me as a child, wavy lines, illegible and nothing at all like what they taught us in school. Who could read those wavy lines, and especially his signature, which I knew was supposed to be his name?

What was the point, I asked him, if no one can read your signature? He just smiled, implying that if you had the secret code you could read that signature. But I didn't have it and he wasn't going to give it to me.

He was proud not only of that signature but of his name itself, which he said meant "Victory of the People," a name that many Hungarian boys of his generation were given, but to my father it was only his name, its meaning profound, proof that he was a leader of greatness.

I must make sure I have special features to set me apart. Without them who will pay attention?

"They used to say I looked like Beethoven!" he said, combing his black hair straight back from his high forehead — a high forehead that was a sign of intelligence, he said, saying my bangs made me look like a monkey and paying me at the age of 12 to grow them out.

Beige, he said, was the best color. And anyone who thought otherwise was missing something.

The way he underlined and marked everything he read. He did not read even the newspaper without a Mont Blanc in hand. As a teenager I looked at the fragments and phrases my father had underlined and questioned him as I had when younger about the signature. "Dad, why did you underline these three words?" His response was again the small smile revealing only that I did not have the secret code.

His instructions: do not bite into your whole piece of bread. Separate and eat it piece by piece. Drink the soup by tilting the spoon sideways. Fold your coat with the lining on the outside when you hang it over a chair at the theater.

When I was ten years old he took me to his office for the day. My mother sent me off dressed in my best party dress, smocking across the chest, a sash that tied behind my waist, puffed sleeves.

On the way, my father stopped at a department store where he asked the sales lady on the quiet carpeted floor to find me a new dress for the occasion. They chose a blue velvet straight shift with a double row of pearl buttons. I'd never worn a straight dress before.

He stopped again to pick up a book for me and left me in the empty conference room — tall leather chairs, long heavy wooden table — with David Copperfield, unabridged, a block of paperback with small print and no pictures. I scraped my way through the pages because there was absolutely nothing else to do except stop every now and then to be introduced to a man in a suit, or a secretary. Then we went home. It took a few years before my mother brought the velvet dress out again. I had needed that much time to grow into it.

TO ENGLAND

"SHALL WE MOVE TO ENGLAND to be with Dad?" my mother asked. It was third grade and my father had gone to England with a new job. I was used to him being away. He always had other things to do.

"Yes!" I said, wondering why this was even a question. Everything was better with Dad.

We move to England in the summer. I am nine. I had been changing schools every year since first grade so this felt familiar. My father was always moving us. Always, he said, for the better.

My father greets us heartily at the airport in London and drives us out to the house he has chosen for us, except that he will only be there on weekends. He will stay in London during the week in an apartment.

And I will go to boarding school.

This is thrilling. I have read about boarding schools. The girls get up in the middle of the night and have feasts. They play tricks on teachers. They are always having fun together. It's like the orphanage I went to once with my mother to deliver sleds from my Brownie troop. My mother left me in the car while she went in with the sleds. I looked up at the orphanage building and thought how fun it must be to live there. A little like the hotels my father was always going to except just for kids.

I go to the boarding school. Quickly there are friends. They are perfect. We play Addams Family in the evenings and then move on to jacks, playing over and over on the floor until we are champions. During holiday breaks we exchange thick letters. I take to the school culture easily – you put your uniform on a chair beside your bed at night, the uniform that requires two pairs of underpants, an outer and an inner. You sit in the same place in the same pew in chapel, at least once a day. You eat at the same table with the same eight girls for each meal, wolfing down fried bread at breakfast, mashed potatoes and sausages at lunch, cups of tea and Nutella at teatime, and slices of roast beef on Sundays. You know the secret nicknames of the 22 nuns. You know the rules – no running in the corridors – and the punishments. And then Latin, French, needlework, handwriting, hockey, music, netball and playing house inside the rhododendron bushes.

At night the movement of the school goes quiet. A nun paces up and down the creaky corridor, making sure we are not talking. It's when I lie in the darkness that I miss my mother. If you cry you have to do it silently so no one can hear you.

Once a month my parents and two little sisters come see me for the weekend. I wait for them in the wood-paneled alcove with the built-in seat. You can look out the leaded panes and see when someone drives up to the front door. I would rather stay where I am, with my friends here in school, doing the things we do. My father takes us to lunch in a restaurant and then we go for a walk outside, probably at a Roman ruin. It is cold and overcast and I am happy to return to the rhythms of the convent. I am separate now from my mother and my little sisters, the way my father is.

REPORT CARD

MY FATHER STOPPED ME on the landing outside his room and asked me to come inside, that he had something important to discuss with me. "Your report card arrived yesterday," he said gravely. "It was not too bad, and it was not too good."

I was home for the first time since September. This was my first report card from the convent boarding school with the 22 nuns and the 250 girls in school uniforms and English accents. It was not like my father to be so serious.

He sat in his armchair and I stood to his right. He held a long piece of white paper. I could see over his shoulder that it was divided by narrow black lines into horizontal rectangular boxes stacked one on top of the other. In each box I could see handwriting, different handwriting in each box.

"Well," said my father, "it says here that you were ranked Number 22 out of the 24 girls in your class."

Ranked? What was that?

And then he began to read, starting at the top. He read slowly. The teachers were critical, saying that I didn't try, that I was slap dash.

I hadn't known they'd been watching me.

I held back the rush of tears, hard, so that my throat hurt.

My father did not look at me. He looked down at the paper and read, subject by subject, teacher by teacher, stretching it all out. "Marta is a smart girl, but makes no effort to fulfill her potential," wrote one teacher.

"Daddy, it says I'm smart!"

"But that you make no effort," he corrected me.

I'd never had a bad report card before. School had always been too easy.

In fact, at this same convent school they had moved me up into the next grade within two weeks of my getting there. That's where I had found my friends – Lucy Ann and Nicola and Madeleine and Ann.

In the new classroom with the older girls the teacher had said I had to have a fountain pen. I could buy one from her, she said – either a black one or a red one. I had money because my father gave me some at the beginning of the term. He didn't give it to me, he gave it to the nuns. Every Friday you went up to a nun behind a desk and told her how much you needed for the following week mostly for the candy that Sister Antony sold on weekends at a little folding table in the doorway of a tiny storage room. Weekend afternoons were devoted to lying on our beds with said candy and a book from the library that was only open on Saturdays, books that had nothing to do with God or fancy literature. Some weeks you might want to also buy something special, like a holy card from the holy shop. Or this business of needing a pen. I picked the red one and learned to fill it from the white china cup of ink embedded in my wooden desk. And one evening as I sat doing math homework another teacher passed by and noticed I was adding and subtracting fractions by drawing circles and dividing them up like slices of pie, the way my mother had shown me once. "Oh my goodness," she had flustered. "We have to show you the proper way!"

My father continued on to the next subject, making sure I heard every mean word.

I didn't know what they wanted, how to be different, how to change anything.

I just knew that when we played dress-up on Saturday afternoons I always wanted to wear the man's jacket with the long coattails. And I had learned to play chopsticks on the beat-up piano in the playroom.

And my father read on while tears piled up in my throat like rocks as I waited for when he said I could go.

HELGA

IT WAS CHRISTMAS VACATION and they said I would fly by myself to meet my father in Switzerland. I had never flown by myself. I was eleven. I was home from the boarding school I had been going to for a couple of years and we were still living in England.

I was handed over to a nice stewardess who, in turn, handed me over to my father at the Geneva airport who greeted me with his usual jubilation.

He brought me to a hotel and together we walked through our two assigned rooms. As we passed through the adjoining bathroom, I pointed to a large white basin next to the toilet and asked what it was.

"It's for ladies to wash their wee-wee holes in," my father said. I kept going, escaping into the next moment as quickly as possible.

The next day we drove out to the mountains. He had an apartment there now, he said, with the joy and pleasure he always produced when showing me his latest thing. The apartment was in a tall skyscraper surrounded by mountains, everything covered in deep snow. Like everything he chose, he presented the building and its surroundings as the best possible place in the world.

We had dinner downstairs in the kind of lavish restaurant my father always favored. It was his natural habitat. A woman called Helga joined us for dinner. Her blonde hair was short and feathered, her eyes bright blue. She wore things like jewelry and dresses and high heels and makeup. She was that kind of lady, not like my mother.

My father sat at the head of the table, Helga to his right, I to his left. I knew, because my father had taught me, that the person to the right was the most important. I knew that this Helga was sitting where my mother should be sitting.

I watched my father tease her, reaching out, laughing, and tracing his forefinger down her nose, saying that it was just like a ski jump. They laughed, but I didn't think her nose looked like a ski jump. In fact, my father's comment felt false to me, as if he'd rehearsed the line.

Later in the meal, Helga asked me with a smile, "Would you ever marry a black man?"

"I'll marry whoever I want," I said and they both laughed.

My father took me to a hairdresser. The ladies fussed over me and ultimately delivered me back to my father with two pigtails. They had wrapped black velvet bands over the elastic bands that kept the pigtails in place. My father enthusiastically bought several sets of these black velvet bands, all of which disappeared, along with the Mont Blanc pen and the Omega watch he had also given me, adult things that made no impression and disappeared into boarding school life.

The day before we were flying back to England, my father and I sat down for lunch, back in Geneva, at Helga's house, a big dark place, with a lot of furniture and carpets. Like the fancy restaurants, this was the kind of house my father liked. With delight he pointed out how Helga could press a button with her foot to summon the maid.

I pretended not to see the wrapped gift that lay next to my napkin. Clearly, it was meant for me, but I could not think of a polite way to acknowledge it. Finally, Helga and my father urged me to open it. It was a small folder made of leather with "Passport" stamped in gold. I could tell from the adults' faces that this was something to be very happy about. But, again, it did not feel like something that had anything to do with me, with my life with the friends back in boarding school where we played horses and shared any information we could find about sex.

In the big black taxi after the airplane I goofed around with my father. I was feeling a burst of confidence and was pretending to be a grown-up, the kind of lady he might meet at a party. My father laughed and played along as if I were doing a great job of impersonation. Stepping up my game, I let the name "Mikki" come out of my mouth, the name Helga called him. The syllables immediately felt gross and frightening on my tongue. I had gone too far into somewhere I didn't want to be. I stopped playing.

MEAN MADELEINE

"I HAVE A BONE TO PICK WITH YOU," said Madeleine.

We were lying under two adjacent beds in someone's dorm, hiding, some game going on. We were 12, except she was 13.

I'd never heard someone say "a bone to pick with you," but Madeleine was the grown-uppiest in our fivesome so it was normal for her to say things the rest of us didn't. She had short brown hair and light freckles and rabbity teeth.

She was grown-uppy especially because she knew how to put on a play because her parents did plays all the time in the faraway place where she lived during school vacations so when we did a play here in school she knew everything we needed and that's why we put on two plays in front of the whole school by ourselves, writing everything and acting them and getting props and costumes.

I had never heard that phrase before, but I could tell it was mean in a nasty, removed, serious kind of way. She had never talked mean to me before. Nobody had. The five of us had been perfect friends.

Madeleine usually came first in our class. That was another sort of grown-uppy thing about her. Every Friday a slip of white paper with all our names typed in a column was posted by the door of the classroom, everybody ranked in order of how well they had done that week. My friends and I were usually in the top bunch, but Madeleine usually had the very first spot.

Of my four main friends, I admired Nicola's ability to draw and the way her body had so much elasticity as she leapt across the floor on hands and crepe-soled shoes, impersonating a horse as if she knew something about horses that no one else did. She could draw them like an adult, like no other kid could possibly. Plus, she was completely unafraid when we went riding, even when she got bucked off the Arab who no one else was trusted to ride. I was scared every week, but pretended I loved riding so that I would be more like Nicola. Who also had really good handwriting and was good at music.

Lucy Ann liked riding too. Lucy Ann was very pretty but her best thing was how she could sing better than anyone else in the school except Sister Barbara. Lucy Ann was always invited to sing solos when we did special choir things for chapel.

And Lucy Ann had divorced parents and went out to movies during Christmas break so she too had a life I wished for.

Ann was my official best friend, but I was more her best friend than she was mine. I liked her, but she was not exciting. She was very good at everything boyish. Sometimes I wished Lucy Ann was my official best friend. Nicola and Madeleine were a couple as were Ann and I. Most of the time the couples thing didn't matter except as an almost invisible structure.

"I have a bone to pick with you," said Madeleine, no smile.

It seemed I had done something very very wrong. I had said I would share a dorm with Jane and Sheila. The bad thing I had done, said Madeleine, was that I was leaving Ann behind in the cubicles, my best friend. How could I?

I hadn't thought of it like that. Sheila and Jane had pulled me aside two evenings ago after dinner when we were all in the hall, the giant room where we could almost do whatever we wanted until bedtime, and they had asked me if I'd like to move out of the cubicles and into a dorm with them, and I had said yes because in the moment it had sounded daring and new, but the next morning I had had a sense of foreboding and wished I could take back my promise, but how do you take something like that back?

"So mean," said Madeleine grimly from underneath the bed.

She and Nicola stopped talking to me. Put me in Coventry. Lucy Ann faintly followed suit. Not Ann so much, but Ann was not so important.

During the next set of holidays, I asked my mother if I could switch schools. I did not say why, of course. I spoke to her as I was playing jacks, she in another room. All very casual. "Can I change schools, Mum?"

"Sure."

They switched my school. I thought everything would be okay then, like all the other schools I'd been to when it was always not fun for a little bit in the beginning, but then you made friends and off you went. But it was not like that this time. I couldn't break through from feeling like the new awkward person at the edge of the circle. It was horrifying. I had become one of the people I had observed in the past, a wallflower, like my mother.

BLACKHEADS

ONE SATURDAY MORNING my father says I have blackheads in my ear and they have to come out. I've read about blackheads and what to do about them in the magazine I get every month called Jackie that is all about girls who are teenagers and have boyfriends.

I didn't know my father even knew about blackheads.

When I was little, if he was home, he treated our cuts and scrapes by making us sit down while he examined the wound. He made a long slow ceremony out of his ministrations. If my mother were the one dealing with a hurt she put a Band-Aid where it was needed and you were back in the fray, but my father made you stop. You just had to wait until he was done. "First, the yellow powder," he said each time with a smile that knew you were impatient to get back to what you were doing but that he had the power to make you sit still. He sprinkled yellow powder from its brown metal cannister on any broken skin as if it were his personal magic potion for solving all problems.

But blackheads is something new.

He tells me to lie down on his bed. His single bed has a green cover that matches the dark green drapes, the dark green seeming to reflect a somber masculinity. He leans over me, peering into my ear and begins to squeeze a tiny piece of skin as if with fiery pincers.

"Ow!" I yell and jerk my head away.

"Now, now," he says, his eyes not moving from my ear, "keep still," and again he pinches and squeezes. I twist away in pain.

But he will not let me go. My mother hovers in the background not saying yes, not saying no. These blackheads have to be removed as if I have some shameful stain that must not be seen by anyone. He is correcting something that is wrong with me, something I cannot see, but everyone else can. Or maybe only him.

SPECIAL OCCASIONS

A FEW DAYS AFTER WE HAD RETURNED from England to live again in the house we actually owned, the one we had lived in twice before, my father sat me down in the dining room. I was 14 now. He wanted to tell me something. He brought out a brochure and asked me to look at it. With glossy photos and extravagant prose it extolled the benefits of purchasing a certain type of asphalt. My father said that now he was selling this asphalt. He said it as if something wonderful had happened, adding, "I did not make much money last year. Less than $8,000."

I don't know how much $8,000 is, but I know he is talking about the year that he spent alone in Washington DC, while we stayed in England. He'd quit the London job, or it had ended after its flourishing beginning. As always, he blamed the end of a job that had once been a triumph on the stupidity of other people and said that in Washington DC he would become a consultant.

At the dining room table with the glossy brochure, my father's bravado is transparent. Why is he pretending to be happy about selling asphalt? What has that to do with plush offices, personal secretaries, fancy restaurants and business trips to foreign countries? I know my job right now is to echo his delight, but I want to get back upstairs to my radio where "Wake Up Maggie" is playing every hour and I am busy learning this new jeans-wearing country.

I start school where there are boys in every class. I have not been with boys since I was nine. Not only that, but the girls wear a different set of clothes every day. They have endless wardrobes. I do not see the same color corduroys on them for months at a time, while I think long and hard about how to make five different, unrecognizable outfits a week.

And then it is Christmas Eve. That's when I see it. That's when I see that we are poor. There are not enough presents beneath the tree. There is too much space between the boxes. I see it the moment I enter the room.

I do my part by not asking for anything. That's easy. Well, not easy, but I know how to do it. It is second nature.

But while my mother, sisters and I live a penny-counting life, my father goes every Saturday to the opera. He often asks me to go with him and each time I look forward to the trip. The idea of the city, the night, the unexpected. I dress up and sit beside him in the car, each time forgetting that part of the deal is enduring his presence. His endless ongoing lecture on how to live boils me in silent fury.

Soon though we are gliding up the red velvet staircase of the opera house, both of us giving in to the seduction of borrowed luxury. I take little pleasure in the actual music. It is my father's music, which he has already told me is superior to what I listen to. The intermission means coffee and whipped cream confections in the crowded theater café, my father and I now in some kind of rigid dance, my father keeping the smile on his face, a smile that tells me I don't get it – that I am too much like my mother – and although I am sure he is wrong, I am not sure.

AT HOME

I COME FROM MY ROOM in the attic down a steep narrow staircase with walls on either side, the steps carpeted in beige. The beige carpet throughout the house is new and has softened the rough edges of the house that my parents rescued from dereliction when I was very little.

I like the changes my father has imposed here while we were in England. They make the house a little more worldly, a little more like other people's houses, though not really. It will never be an American house with a finished basement or a kitchen island or a freezer packed with months of food. I have seen these things in other houses belonging to kids who invited me over once because we were friends in third grade, but I didn't understand much of what they talked about and took for granted, and the visits weren't repeated. I'm on my own. There is some comfort in the new rose trellis, the two-car garage, the paved driveway – they help us appear a little less off-culture.

I climb down from my private world in the attic to the second floor where my mother has a room and each of my two sisters. Their rooms are not carpeted, the dark wide boards from another century with thick square-headed nails left exposed. I know my mother has always liked these old boards.

And down another narrow steep carpeted staircase to the living room. My father has installed a slim pair of French doors at the bottom of these stairs, delicate white wooden frames of glass. It's a tight fit. The little French doors don't really belong here, but he closes them at night, sealing off the downstairs for himself. He sleeps down here, in the new front hall with its new couch that opens into his bed each night. He is not the daddy with airline tickets anymore. He is the dad who drives to the city and back every day in the Ford Grenada, green with beige interior, colors that match the Mercedes in his mind.

When I walk through the living room on my way to the kitchen each school morning my father is standing in his underpants, buttoning a white shirt fresh from the dry cleaner. I smell Listerine with the steam from his bath. There is classical music emanating from his stereo tucked into the tall piece of dark furniture pressed against one wall. My father calls this piece of furniture of glass and wood "the armoire." The top half has delicate glass doors that open onto shelves holding mementos from my father's recent years – brass and silver objects from Morocco and a small enameled antique pill box inscribed with the words, "I am yours while life endures." Helga gave that to him. He keeps his gall bladder stones in it. "WQXR," intones the somber male voice of the radio announcer, "the radio station of The New York Times."

I push open the swing door to the kitchen. It closes behind me. Here too WQXR is going though this time from a beige plastic radio I remember from earliest childhood. My mother has three paper-bag lunches lined up on the counter. She is boiling eggs, popping toast.

I sit at the end of the small wooden table. This is also my father's place. We share it, never eating in the kitchen at the same time. He is usually alone when he eats here. The only time my father eats with us is on weekends, for lunch, and we do that out in the dining room, at the dark wooden table with matching chairs, all related to the armoire in the living room.

My father said he bought these pieces of furniture as birthday presents for my mother, but they didn't arrive until his birthday. He had shown me how each chair-leg ended with a carved claw clutching a ball. There was something significant about this, a symbol of something that, he implied, reflected well upon the owner of such a chair. These things gave him joy, a security that he had the right things. Almost. If only he could get all the things and put them in the right place and have the right wife and the right children.

We sit at the dining room table for lunch on Saturdays and Sundays eating our largest meals of the week, my mother at the end nearest the kitchen, my father at the other end, my sisters and I scattered between. The table is made up of two halves that are supposed to fit neatly together with the help of pegs on one side pushed into holes on the other. But the holes do not grip the pegs tightly enough and the seam down the middle of the table is forever coming apart. Each time we sit down to eat we begin by pushing the two halves of the table together so that the crack down the middle disappears and we think maybe this time it will hold, but it never does. By the end of each meal the separation has reappeared.

The tensions rise and fall — my father trying for conversation sometimes with pedantic retellings of history, sometimes by teasing us, which is excruciating, his attempts at humor that make my sisters and me squirm because we cannot shut him up without being rude. The worst is when the parents fight or start brewing one. This I cannot bear. This I step into, as if into a dog fight, deflecting, pretending there is no fight, finding ways to bounce the conversation in other directions.

I can never bear their fighting, am on alert for its simmering that threatens to break through the surface, knowing that even my father's compliments about the salad dressing mask hostility. I can tell because they are so repetitive. And anger is not allowed here. My father has made that very clear. And yet my mother's anger boils over so regularly that we have all learned to watch for every change in tone that could signal an explosion aimed at one of us kids or, usually late at night, at my father. The sound of their voices coming up from the living room keeps me awake — hers at an out-of-control pitch, his tight and low, attempting to appease and avoid.

One morning, my father and I were both sitting at the breakfast table, an unusual formation. We were about to go into the city together. My mother was going at him in the background, every word she spoke perfectly designed to make him explode. I kept silent as if this weren't happening. What else to do with the boiling inside of me? My father too kept buttering his toast, sipping his instant coffee and telling her quietly it was delicious. In the car, coming down the driveway, my father said, "You handled that very well."

FRIENDS WITH STRANGERS

I LIKED STRANGERS. I liked people who did not know me. I liked standing by the side of the road with my thumb out, getting into a car, usually with a man by himself, and then I could play the part of the girl in my head, the girl who was free, who traveled like it was nothing, who didn't go to high school and didn't need anyone. The girl I really am could not be of interest to anybody. But the man driving doesn't have to know that there are two of us. He can think what I tell him to think. He can see a girl who calls the shots and goes where she pleases. After all, I am not with him for long.

Sometimes, instead of staying in my attic room in the afternoon, I walked down the short steep driveway, then along the road for a few minutes before turning and putting out my thumb, transforming from a schoolgirl into a heroine. Not that there was much traffic here. Just a car every now and then. Still, it was enough. Someone always stopped. I always got in. A few rides and I'd be home for dinner in the kitchen with my mother and two little sisters, the wooden table pushed up against the stove with two or three saucepans – broccoli, potatoes, a pork chop with applesauce.

How on earth do you get out of your life? When would I ever be out of this house, on my own, living in the worlds I was sure were waiting for me? I could see those worlds in the songs on the radio, in the long looping lyrics of Dylan. I could see myself with many lovers, a beautiful admired woman, an artist, free. I saw no worry in those future scenes, no trouble. Or if there was trouble it was like trouble in a book. Interesting, something to watch, not something with its hands around my throat.

Although I was stuck at home and stuck in school, there was no excuse not to be nailing the boy part. The first part of boys was easy, getting their attention. It happened by itself. Boys were always looking and they always noticed me. But then what? I did not know how the rest could possibly happen. How would a boy ever stop looking at every pretty girl and stay with me instead? This seemed impossible.

But in the songs and in the books they stayed. There, boys really loved one girl. In real life, I'd have to be an acrobat to keep their attention. I'd have to be fabulous, brilliant and always beautiful every single second. Somehow. The future me would have that figured out. Otherwise, she couldn't exist.

WALDORF ASTORIA

MY MOTHER TOOK ME TO MACY'S because I needed a dress. We did not shop often. When we did, it was to get one thing. A sweater or a pair of shoes, purchases that were made when they were deemed unavoidable.

It had not always been like this, but it decidedly was now. So going to Macy's for a dress was a thing. My father was having an event in the city to present his book to the public. I hadn't read his book although I had copy-edited the footnotes. It was a maze of economic and political theory, as dry as a bone from what I could tell. He'd paid a man on Long Island to publish it. My father had dreamed out loud about a cover with a picture of the globe and a dove and an olive branch, but the cover came out plain navy blue with white block printing. My father did not complain. He arranged an evening of cocktails and then dinner, all at the Waldorf Astoria, a place to feel rich in. I was to attend. My mother would come in by train just for the dinner, and my two little sisters would not be there at all.

It was summertime and my tan was deep, my hair long and dark. I tried on a yellow halter dress and fell quite in love with the image in the mirror, silently accepting the murmurs of approval from two motherly types as my natural due.

The cocktails part of the celebration was held in a tastefully furnished suite, my father and I standing at the door, my father greeting everyone heartily. I didn't know these people – men in suits, women in jewelry and purses – my father's daytime people. A few times he'd invited some couple or other out to our house in rural suburbia for Sunday lunch. Conversation would be stilted. My father would insist my sisters and I play our half-practiced piano pieces. The same couple never came twice. The Waldorf Astoria suite was full of people like this.

I felt like an ornament, standing beside my father. I assumed he wanted me there because I was a better female attachment than my mother who had been taken over by middle age and slips that showed.

Dinner was held in a large room with round tables, white tablecloths, waiters, and a podium up front at which my father stood to speak. His opening joke wafted slowly to the floor, unbuoyed by the responsive, supportive laughter it was supposed to release. His prepared talk struggled on.

Afterwards, the people gone, it was just me and my parents in the abandoned room, broken bread rolls on the white tablecloths, scattered bits of heavy silverware and crumpled linen napkins.

As we threaded our way to the exit I saw a piece of paper balled up on a table. I knew it held something. I reached for it. "When is this guy going to shut up?" read the note.

I left the paper on the table and caught up with my parents. We didn't talk much on the way home. We never did.

DETROIT

I GET THE IDEA IN MY ATTIC BEDROOM. It's where I got all my ideas. The attic bedroom, perched at the top of the house above the rest of the family, was my world.

On the bottom floor was my father, nursing his whiskey and soda in a chunky glass, sitting in the well stuffed armchair covered in a coarsely woven fabric depicting sunflowers. He sat there alone, after his solo dinner in the kitchen, Beethoven or Mozart on the Fisher stereo, perhaps Iris Murdoch or Somerset Maugham in his hand.

Upstairs on the second floor slept my mother and two younger sisters, each in their own room. And I had the top floor under the pitched roof, the space divided in two, as close to an apartment as my 16-year-old self was going to get.

The main room that held my stereo, desk and couch cushions was my land of possibility. There were no friends calling. I had lost the knack for instant friendship when I was 12. I had become suddenly almost unable to speak, crushed by everyone else's seeming ease.

In my attic room, with its steeply sloping ceiling, I could be alone with no one seeing this embarrassing isolation. The DJ's on WPLJ couldn't see it. They spoke to me in their low brooding voices and played our music — songs with guitars, sung by men with ponytails, girls in long dresses, songs that wove stories that I followed attentively, songs of being on the road, in love, getting high, getting in trouble.

I wanted that world. I wanted to step into those songs. I wanted to be in the cab of the 18-wheeler with Bobbie McGee, I wanted to be on the Marrakesh Express with the boy who would sing about it later, I wanted to be sittin' downtown in a railway station one toke over the line.

I had to get out of where I was. This high school was useless. I would never find my people here, especially not the boys with guitars and moustaches and ponytails. They weren't here in the fluorescent corridors, not in the classrooms of desks that had their chairs attached to them. There were boys here, even some I wished would notice me, but they did not. Their eyes did, but these boys did not call me or walk to class with one arm slung across my hips. I stayed in my silence and aloneness and wished for other things.

I have to hitchhike. I have to stand by the highway with a big piece of cardboard in my hands that says IOWA or CALIFORNIA. I must show the world who I really am, and then my people will see me, welcome me in. I'll be able to talk then.

I work with what I have. Negotiate with parents. Get a Greyhound bus pass good anywhere for a month. I will go see my grandmother on the other side of the continent in British Columbia. My father drives me as far as Ann Arbor, puts me on a bus headed to Detroit, waves, and finally I am free.

I get off in Detroit. It is early morning. I have a small knapsack left over from childhood, but at least it's a backpack of some sort, essential for telegraphing who I am, as important as the patches on my jeans.

I walk out of the bus station. I have a couple of hours until the next bus leaves for the Canadian border. I am not quite sure, now that I am actually here, how to do this. I thought it would feel different, but I feel like the same person I always am. The people and worlds I want to be part of are just as out of reach. How far do I have to go to get there?

I walk to a city park, green with summer. A man starts talking to me. He has an accent, his skin is a little darker than mine. He is much older than me. His clothes are shabby and he has a tooth or two missing.

He is friendly. He smiles and says nice things like how beautiful I am.

The boys in the songs always think the girls they love are beautiful. This man is not a boy from one of my songs, but neither is he from my high school. He likes me and I drink in the brightness of his brown excited eyes.

We sit on the grass and kiss and kiss. I like kissing very much.

He jumps up with enthusiasm and says he has to show me the zoo. It's not far, he says, just a few stops on the city bus. No, I don't want to go. I want to be able to find my way back to the Greyhound station whenever I want.

"Oh, you have to come," he pleads. "It is so close, you will love it. Please!"

I don't want to be a scaredy cat. I want to be an adventuress. That's why I am here. I want to be that girl who is not afraid of anything, who will go anywhere.

"Okay," I say.

We board a city bus. The man is so happy. One stop, two stops, three stops. "We're very close," he says, but I don't like it. We're getting too far from the bus depot.

I jump off at the next stop. The man is at my side. He is sad I will not go further with him. We walk back to the bus depot and I climb aboard my Greyhound. I look out the window. The man is waving from the sidewalk, all smiles. He has tied a piece of string around his finger. "Don't forget me!" he is saying, pointing to the string. "Don't forget me!"

OFF TO SCHOOL

MY FATHER HAD A THING for one Ivy League school in particular. He had found a place there in the early 50s, a Hungarian immigrant, almost no English, so little English and so much despair at the comedown of refugee status that he had tried to overdose on sleeping pills.

That was just around the time when he was meeting my mother. And I can see how she saw him: handsome, not another football-playing jock, a cultured European who needed her.

Somehow he had found his way into the prestigious college, getting a Masters there in Economics to add to a PhD from Hungary. I never did learn the step-by-step of how that happened. He wove the institution into his story so deftly that I didn't realize there might be a seam there. Listening to my father tell it, you just assumed he was brilliant and this college had come running after him.

He always held the school up as the only one in America worth its salt. I absorbed its name in the air I breathed, even as I had no interest, I thought, in doing anything my father wanted.

And now, eleventh grade, everyone around me was applying to colleges. College wasn't a maybe in my house. It was an assumption, though neither parent knew anything about the all-American process.

The school library had a paperback book listing every college in the country. It was about six inches thick. It stared at you from its perch on a waist-high bookcase at the library's entrance, impossible to miss.

I spent my lunchtimes in the library perusing the encyclopedic volume as if I were planning a vacation. This was my big chance. I was finally going to be on my own, out of my parents' domain. Whatever I picked had to be good. It had to be stepping into the world that would change everything, a world that would release me from the prison I was trapped in, the prison that had turned me into a girl who couldn't even enter the cafeteria because it would show her up as having no one to sit and laugh with.

Shielded by a three-sided library carrel, I looked at the five-paragraph descriptions of Berkeley and Antioch. Berkeley's anti-establishment promise needed no introduction, plus it was as geographically far away as I could get. That was good. Antioch had had riots in the 60s. Excellent. And the University of Michigan at Ann Arbor beckoned. I had driven through the campus once and seen houses with big porches, girls in peasant blouses and jeans-made-into-skirts and long-haired boys sitting on the steps. I wanted to be sitting there too.

Whatever school I chose, I wanted throngs of blue-jeaned boys with beards and ponytails, so many I could get lost amongst them, so many that all semblance of this current high school and home life would be blotted out, forgotten forever and I would sail away away away.

My father only wanted me to go to the one school he esteemed. He arranged a visit to the campus with the man he always spoke of with utmost respect, his mentor. I knew, I could feel it, that, like a thousand times before, my father wanted to show me to someone. It was a double helix. It meant that he thought I did the job of being displayed well. It also meant that I had to do the job of being displayed well, that I was on a tightrope of hit or miss.

My father liked to insist that our family was great, that we were the best, said with such deliberation and bravado that you knew we had to overcome feeling that we were actually lesser-than, dependent on the good opinion of those who really had the strength and character and talent and wealth. Like this mentor we were going to see.

I wore the long red corduroy skirt and the embroidered peasant blouse. I felt pretty and therefore prepared. My father introduced me with brightness and cheer.

But the old man in a suit behind the desk was European and I could tell my usual charms made little impression. He did not light up at the sight of my pretty face, instead asking, "What do you want to major in? What interests you in life? What do you want to accomplish with this writing you want to do?" Each question let me know that these vague dreams I had were but watercolors, easily washed away. The people he dealt with already had a firm grasp on such things as route and direction.

We did not stay long.

VIENNA

I MEET MY FATHER IN VIENNA, in the large bright lobby of The Intercontinental Hotel. I am 17. I wear a short cotton halter dress and white sandals with cork heels. My father wears a suit and tie, his black hair pushed straight back and away from his broad forehead and very blue eyes. We meet up with delight, both of us matching in this moment of summer and luxury. In that moment of greeting we are the perfect couple.

I am coming from a month in Hungary spent in a camp for foreign high school kids of Hungarian heritage. And before that, from a couple of weeks traveling through Europe on a train with a backpack still looking for the other people with backpacks. There had been adventures – like smuggling a plastic envelope of cocaine through British customs for the boys I'd met on a ferry – but still somehow I had always felt alone and outside of the world I was looking for.

I have been a student in a small Hungarian town, supposedly studying Hungarian language, history and culture. I haven't learned much. Mostly, I have walked alone into the town where there is a small shop that sells English-language books and I have bought Ulysses and am trying to make my way through it.

But even more, I have been negotiating my days housed with a bunch of fellow teenagers – four in a room – through meals and classes, crushes, alliances and jealousies. There was one boy the first night. We went on a walk together. He was not a hippie. He was my age, a brown-eyed boy. I'd never met a boy like him before, nice, kind, friendly. It was easy, even fun, to be with him. But in the morning I froze. I could not talk to him. I saw myself pretend I didn't know who he was. I just did not know what you are supposed to do once you like someone and they like you. It would fall apart. I was sure it would. I had to crush it quickly before he changed his mind and turned away. I saw the bewilderment and anger in his eyes as I looked past him in the dining room, but I could not stop myself.

After the month of trying to make me more of a Hungarian, I take the train to Vienna to play grown up with my father who is all too happy, it seems in this moment of lobby greeting, to play with me. I do this opening move so nicely, knowing that I am all that my mother isn't. For a moment, I can play the casual beauty, the traveler, the sophisticate, as smooth as an ice skater, no glitches, all truth buried, no need for it here, just appearances. Appearances I can do. For a few moments. I always hope I can keep it going and going as required, but it doesn't take long for me to droop and lose my way. That impenetrable confidence disintegrates and I become desperate for solitude, desperate to escape that solitude.

THE SLENDER THREAD

IN HIGH SCHOOL, when I started reading grown-up books, when I found one I really liked, I gave it to my father for Christmas or a birthday. My mother read as much as my father did, but I did not bring her my literary finds. I did not trust her to feel the poetry of writing the way I did.

It always made my father happy to receive a book from me. He always read it. And though we did not get into long conversations about it, I could tell he appreciated and enjoyed what I had brought. It was one tiny place where we overlapped.

And later, when I began to write, I took my best writings to him. With these, he was always enthusiastic, telling me specifically the sentences or phrases that he had liked.

I did not show my mother my writing with the same expectations. She too would be positive, but in a more general way, not as if she had perceived what I had written as I had intended it. She was likely to put a peculiar spin on it, as if I had written something completely different.

My father and I. Even as we did not agree on anything else as the years piled up, even as his company reduced me to silent fury as if I were in a cobweb and could not fight my way out, still, this slender thread was there, a delicacy in him that was not so obvious in my mother, even as she proved, in the long run, to be the one I could depend on.

PART TWO

LETTER

HE ENGULFS ME, THIS BOY who started things off by sending a long dense letter, typed and single-spaced, that I read in my attic room where the air is close and warm and smells of wood in summer. The sanctuary I want to escape from more than anywhere else in the world.

I hold this letter from the boy in the writing class that I go to Wednesday nights, driving by myself in my mother's green VW station wagon the two hours there and the two hours back, the driving an ecstasy, dancing between lanes, zipping through tolls until I arrive at a basement classroom with a long table and the rough-edged teacher at its head.

I don't like teachers, but I like this one. He seems like a real person, someone I'd like to know if I were anywhere near his league. He's no goody-goody. He does not play teacher. He doesn't smoke or drink in class, but you can tell he does otherwise, and when one night he reads his own screenplay out loud there is so much real life in it that it makes me feel naïve.

It is a prestigious college. It is not the one I go to during the year. It is the college my father has always hoped I would attend, but I did not get in. As a second-best option, he suggested that I take a summer course there. I had looked at the catalog and seen this writing seminar. For once, my father and I wanted the same thing.

The teacher makes me laugh. It's part of why I like these Wednesday evenings. He makes all of us laugh. And when I laugh my eyes keep meeting the dark eyes of a laughing boy across the table. We talk after class, sitting outside for a few minutes. He says he has written a novel.

A novel.

He tosses that out almost as if it's nothing. I want to have written a novel. I want to be writing a novel. I want to be writing, to be a real writer, and look, this boy with a ponytail has already done it.

And then this letter comes from him, typed, single-spaced on crinkly paper. It's not a baby letter. It's a strong letter with long sentences and complex words and then he ends it by writing: I love you.

Suddenly my summer is on fire!

I hold this letter as if it is a magic carpet, promising another world if I don't blow it, a world where I can be a different person, finally.

DINNER

THE BOY IN THE WRITING CLASS has invited me for dinner. He invited me last week when we met in the library. I had been wearing the yellow cotton smock on purpose. I'd made it myself. Not on a machine. I don't know how to use those. But with a needle and thread, the way I learned in convent school.

A smock, to me, is the perfect shirt – it spells hippie, guitars, being on the road. Along with my long hair and jeans it lets you know who I am. Of course, it didn't come out as perfectly as the picture on the sewing pattern promised, but it's still my best shirt.

When he asked me for dinner he asked me what I would like him to make. I did not know any answer to that. I did not know the name of anything. What do girls say when boys ask them this? But I had heard of eggplant parmesan. My friend Ruth had once mentioned it. So I said, "How about eggplant parmesan?"

And now I am ringing the buzzer at a door in a stairwell. The boy flings it open, dark long hair, curly and frizzy, a red terrycloth bathrobe with a blue stripe. He laughs, says he is running behind and leads me, talking, to the end of a corridor.

The apartment is one large room. An electric typewriter sits on a small desk tucked into an alcove by the door, a shelf of plants is lit by a long tube of lavender light suspended over a lumpy brown couch covered in books and papers. In one corner sits an unmade bed, big enough for two. I sit on its edge and it responds with a sloshing sound, tipping me a little to the side. "Sorry," the boy laughs. "Waterbed." There is a long line of red plastic crates filled with records. There's a small TV on top of one of the red cartons and a telephone with a long cord tossed among the sheets. Across the room I see a tiny stove, a counter and sink, a scrap of kitchen. He has everything.

A green plant hangs by the window, trailing vines of leaves, as if the boy has lived here for a long time, as if he has lived with plants and water-beds and his own TV for a long time.

I pull a curtain across my life, across my twin bed in my parents' house, across my parents and my handful of records, across the way I do not get phone calls. There are so many things he must not see.

The boy has changed into jeans and a faded turquoise cotton smock, a wonderful smock, soft, wrinkled, worn, just as it should be.

He asks if I'd like a hit from the bong. I have not had a hit from a bong before, but I have been longing to find the people who take hits from bongs. Yes, I say. I do not do it quite right and he coaches me, holding a match to the little pile of pot, telling me to cover the hole on the plastic tube until it is filled with smoke, then take it all in and hold it there as long as I can. I do all that. I don't feel much, but it doesn't matter. I am here, in this apartment with a boy who is just as I have imagined for so long.

SEX

WE MEET AT THE INFORMATION BOOTH at Grand Central, a place I already know how to get to, thank God, taking the commuter train in from suburbia. I do not want to ask the boy any questions about navigating New York City. Anything I don't know I will figure out on my own. He mustn't know I don't know every single thing about this city the way he does. He lives here. He has always lived here.

As we stand inside the busy terminal, he says he wants to buy some records. He says that people are saying there's a new Dylan called Bruce-something. "This I have to see," says the boyfriend, laughing.

He buys all three of the new guy's records. At once. Just to see if he will like them. I could never do that. The boy, of course, does not know that I have to save money and wait just to buy one record and can never decide which one to get because there are so many I want. And I could never throw my savings at one record just to see if I liked it. And I could never, ever, buy three of them at once. I do not mention any of this.

Then we go to what he calls a "coffee shop." I think my mother would call it a diner. I ask the waiter for a salami sandwich with slices of raw green pepper. It is not on the menu so the waiter is confused, but says he can figure it out. The boyfriend gets a burger, "very rare," and a coke "with lots of ice." The waiter has no questions about his order.

The boy and I go to his apartment. We lie on his twin bed from childhood and he tells me about his girlfriend in high school, how they once had a phone call that lasted 13 hours and how his last girlfriend used to call up the radio station and ask them to play "Brown-Eyed Girl." The boy likes to reminisce about these other girls. I have no such stories though I mention boys from the past as if I did. And I would never think to call a station to ask for a song and I cannot imagine a boy chuckling years later about my sweetness.

When it starts to get dark I say I have to go home. "Why?" he asks, smiling, as if anyone else could stay all night. I think of my mother. She is expecting me. She will get really mad if I am not home on time. The threat of her fury compels me home.

FINALLY

ANOTHER NIGHT, AT HIS SCHOOL APARTMENT, the one with the waterbed, we were lying side by side for a long time, listening to a Dylan bootleg (a word I'd never heard before). Mostly, I was waiting. He had said in that letter two weeks ago that he loved me. And here we were in perfect kissing position. And yet he did not reach for me. And so I kissed him first and he slipped his hands under my striped shirt, the red and orange one from the thrift store.

"Relax your tongue," he said after a few minutes. And "your breasts are smaller than I thought. I like them." No boy had ever talked to me about my breasts before. They had touched them, but never said anything. That would have been too embarrassing.

And then he had come to my house, mother and sisters away for the week, father living in New York City. Thank goodness I have a father living in the city right now. I get double points for this: parents living separate lives, father in the city. United parents would only add to my provinciality.

My father is renting a room at a club. It's the club of the school that he has in common with the boy. I go to this club once a week to proof a manuscript my father has written. About world economic systems. Anyway, I am grateful for this set-up because it too sounds good: working for a father who is a writer. It makes the point that I have my own reasons, sometimes, to be in Manhattan, a relationship to this city independent of this boy. I wear this badge proudly.

Days after the kiss on the waterbed the boy had taken the train and I had met him in my father's beige VW bug, a car I liked because it was often a hippie car, though my father's version had no signs of hippiedom. The boy sat in the passenger seat and ran his hand up my bare leg. "Didn't take you for a shaver," he laugh-talks.

A girl is supposed to have smooth legs but not shave them. Shaving is gross. So are stubbly legs. You are supposed to keep your shaving well hidden and here I am, discovered. He keeps exposing things I keep hidden, that everyone I've ever known has kept hidden.

I show him my attic room, my almost-apartment. Thank God I have the stereo sitting there on the carpet, casual. Without that, there would be nothing unusual except the couch cushions on the floor which give, perhaps, the impression that friends come over and smoke pot and listen to music with me.

The boy is most interested in my one Dylan album. Dylan is my favorite, his too, but I only have one album. It is a double album. Dylan's "greatest hits." I know every word of every lyric on those two records. I have listened to them over and over, turning over the meaning of each line, following the parade of pictures painted by the songs. I have never thought of my Dylan record as a compilation of songs from other records. I don't know Dylan's other records. But the boyfriend does and he peruses the list of songs on the cover, commenting on the choices made.

He is here and we are alone and we are going to have sex and I have to explain why I don't have a diaphragm. Every girl should have a diaphragm. Because by now no girl should still be a virgin. I say that I left my diaphragm at school.

I cannot imagine having sex in my twin bed up in the attic even though he says he did it that way in high school all the time and that it's fine. I take us to my mother's empty double bed. The boyfriend likes the child portrait of me that hangs over the bed. He sits cross-legged and naked pointing his camera at it so he'll have his own copy. It is wonderful to have a naked boy in the room. Life is finally beginning to happen.

So we have the sex like in the books. Finally, I am no longer an embarrassing virgin. He says that I moan a lot in bed, that he is not sure I am enjoying it. "Don't you want to have an orgasm?" he asks. He shouldn't have mentioned the moans. That's embarrassing. I did them just to sound involved. And an orgasm I hadn't thought about though I like having a boyfriend who can say words like that out loud. "Let's change the sheets," I say.

FAMILY DINNER

I AM TO MEET THE NEW BOYFRIEND'S father and sister. I take the train into Grand Central. I know the way. There is almost nothing I like better than coming into New York City by myself. Walking on the sidewalk, I feel as self-directed and purposeful as everyone else.

The new boyfriend thrills and terrifies me. He is so enthusiastic about this thing he calls "our relationship," but although the unfamiliar words "I love you" that he uses so easily are delicious, they are as scary as a bridge that could fall away beneath me at any moment. How could this boy love me? He must think I am somebody else. I must continue to delude him or he will lose interest. I know this without having to think about it.

Having him as a boyfriend for these few summer weeks has not only finally sent my stubborn virginity packing, it has also given me a boy to be in the city for and with. He never says it directly, but I can tell he feels superior to anyone who has not grown up in Manhattan. I cannot argue. For him, doormen are invisible before and after you say hello to them and walking out for a burger or a movie in the middle of the afternoon is nothing.

So I have a boy with long dark curly/frizzy hair, a boy with a craggy uneven face and a personality unlike other people's. He is not a football star. He is not one of the bland boys from school. He walks with an awkward gait, $20-bills spilling out of his pockets, no wallet, no underwear, no breakfast, tossing aside rules I have never questioned. He answers the phone by saying "hi" flatly instead of "hello" with a question mark, as if he already knows who is there. He has an answering machine with a casual witty message that he changes from week to week. When people say, "How are you?" he says, "Good," instead of "Fine," which is what everyone else says.

I have dressed up for this dinner. I wear a skirt and sandals because I am meeting the boyfriend and his family in a restaurant. You see, if he were meeting my family it would be at my house with my mother's cooking, but when you meet his family it is in a restaurant in New York City, which of course to him is nothing.

The restaurant is a bustling place with a big bar up front and the dining room beyond. It is the kind of place my father likes, a serious place for a serious dinner. Perhaps it is more American than the serene, formal environments that my father favors, but still, it is close and I know my way around.

I look in the dining room, but do not see the boyfriend and so I take a seat at the bar where I sit for what feels like a long time, nursing something in a glass, playing as best I can the part of the casual sophisticate sitting at a bar.

And then he is there, saying they've been there all along and where was I and I glide to the table as smoothly as I can, having, it seems, caused disruption by my failure to find them.

I sit in my skirt, my tucked-in blouse, my clothes from home. The boyfriend's sister is laughing and talking a lot about the vacation abroad she has just returned from and the new diet she is on. The boyfriend teases her because she doesn't have a boyfriend. She shows no sign of being bothered by his laughing jibes, almost agreeing that she must be doing something wrong, speaking of herself almost in third person, as if she were a cute stuffed animal. The father does not say much. He sits, small and dapper and respected, presiding and smoking, the grown-up who will pay for all this. The boyfriend and his sister call him by his first name.

The chatter of the boyfriend and his sister is the energy of the table. I leap from rock to rock as they appear out of the water like sea monsters. I leap quickly, dancing from one word to the next, listening hard, looking for openings, every fiber stretched to be as at home here as the boyfriend and his sister because they make it clear that this is an easy place to be, easy for them and for anyone they like. So I dart and dance to keep up, to be one of them, and they seem to approve although the discrepancy between us is glaring.

ICE CREAM AND BATHTUB

"WE LOOK GOOD TOGETHER," he says, looking into the mirror by the elevator. "Looking good together" is not something I would have checked for or recognized. But every time he says something that means he likes me I am relieved.

We are going out into the night to a new ice cream place he has read about in Time Out. This alone is exciting. That I can walk out at night like this, in the city, asking no one for permission. Alone at home, I'd be in bed by now because there is no reason to stay up. But with the boy everything is different.

It's a short walk up the avenue before we step into the crowded brightly lit space dominated by a long counter. Everyone's heads are tilted up, studying the columns of flavors posted behind the counter. And we choose whatever we want. Not just ice cream, but hot fudge and whipped cream. Everything. He pays for his. I pay for mine. I do not want to be old-fashioned. I don't want "dates" where the man pays for things any more than I want to wear hairspray or paint my nails. I pay for myself. And he does not argue and I like that we are not conventional.

Ice cream in hand, we keep walking northward up Second Avenue, finding ourselves soon inside a little park, a child's playground, and by now there is the softest rain moistening the nighttime summer air.

I start to cry. Just a little. I am not sure why. Except that I can. It feels like I have not cried since I was little and yet there seems to be so much to cry about and his chest feels solid and comforting. What a great feeling, the comfort of his arms around me. I have never been with anyone with whom I can cry. Just to feel his company in these moments when it is suddenly easy to cry is all I want.

He says I am depressed. As if depression were a thing that attaches itself to you and that you can get rid of. He is a Psych major at the college of which my father is so fond. He has a big book that lists every medication and what it does for you. He says he slit his wrists once and stayed in a psych hospital for six months. He wanted to kill himself when his last girlfriend broke up with him. Not only has he written a novel, he has attempted suicide.

I have read One Flew Over the Cuckoo's Nest. I believe in the people that other people say are crazy. But other than that, I have no vocabulary. Not the way he does. A word for everything.

Back in the apartment he suggests we get into the bathtub. We each take one end of the tub, facing each other. He looks at me. I think he likes this more than I do, but I am trying. After all, I am with a boy and we are without clothes. I have finally gotten this far.

He asks me if I think I am more beautiful with my clothes on or off. I know it's a trick question. I know the right answer is "off" so that's the answer I give, but it's not true. I am much prettier with my clothes on.

THE HAPPY PLACE

THE BOYFRIEND INVITES ME for the weekend to be with his family at their beach place. My mother gives me permission. We meet up in the city first with his father and sister and take a cab out of the city where we board a helicopter.

They talk about other things, not the helicopter, and the father, as before, says little. So it's mostly the boyfriend laugh-talking, the sister parrying and me not talking enough, not taking any lead at all, feeling always that I am playing catch-up.

It's a big house with a circular drive. Walking towards the house in the almost-dark, the father already inside, we come across a boy like us. "Hey, Eric, how are you?" asks the boyfriend.

"High," says the other boy and everybody laughs.

"Stepbrother," explains the boyfriend, pulling me towards and into the house and leading me down a couple of corridors into a kitchen the size of two rooms with a long wooden table. Everything inside the house is lush — antiques, carpets, modern paintings and colorful pottery. A small woman in a housedress and flat shoes, her black hair pulled into a bun, is arranging food on platters under the direction of a pretty woman with longish un-brushed henna-red hair. She's dressed in a beachy caftan-type gown and holds a cigarette.

"Hey," says the boyfriend, depositing a kiss on her freckled cheek and introducing me. This is Kitty, the father's wife but not the boyfriend's mother. She smiles, but not broadly. Her narrow brown eyes assess me, calculating something.

"Hi," she says. "I put you two at the top of the second stairs, next to the blue room."

"Great!" says the boyfriend and we move swiftly back through the antiques and modern artwork, up to a third floor and our room with a slanted ceiling, small but luxurious, a thick new comforter on the bed and matching plump pillows.

As always, I wake up early in the morning. The boyfriend sleeps. I wait. I read. I wait. An hour. Two hours. He still sleeps. I get up. The house is quiet even though there are many people staying here. I met them at dinner, people who laughed and smoked and were all so happy to be here. I walk to the beach on the other side of a lawn where croquet is set up. I walk as long as I can along the empty sand and crashing waves, a place I would exult in if I didn't have this strange world to return to. I walk back to it. The big house is still quiet and the boyfriend has not stirred.

I don't get this place, feel even frightened beyond the boy's protective shadow, hoping hard as we finally go through the day amongst the others that I am performing well. Until the next day when, alone in the bedroom, he says, "You're so quiet. You never talk. Let's play the truth game. Each person has to say something that is true. My last girlfriend and I used to play it all the time." I freeze. Freeze that he has called me out. Freeze that I have to speak the truth.

Can I even say it? Can I even say that I want to be back in the city by ourselves, going out to a coffee shop for a hamburger again, wrapped in the red padded booth with nothing to think about except the ice cream sundae to come? But we're playing the truth game so I have to say it. I want to leave.

"Really?" he asks. "You don't like it here?"

I fumble. Say something.

"Well, we can go back, I guess," he says. "I heard someone is looking for someone to drive their car back to the city so maybe we could do that. But you need to tell my father."

Tell his father? Well, okay, if that's what one does. His father is almost always in his room even as other people are scattered on the lawn or reclining with drinks. I find the father sitting on his bed, legs outstretched, watching golf and smoking. "Hi," I say. "I think I'd like to go back to the city. I'm just not feeling that good here."

"Okay, sweetheart," he replies, hardly taking his eyes from the screen.

"See you soon," and we give each other a peck on the cheek. And I half feel like a daughter and half I feel invisible.

And then the boy and I are speeding on the highway in a red Triumph, the top down, me at the wheel and I am joyous. I am alone with the boy again, his hand on my thigh. Tonight we will get Kung Pao chicken with peanuts, and ice cream, and his arms will be around me as we fall asleep with Van Morrison floating into the mystic. Is this how things work? You say what you want and then it happens?

THE BREASTS

I AM IN THE BOYFRIEND'S APARTMENT. It is the one where he grew up. He only comes here now when he is not at school. No one lives in it anymore. His mother went back to Mississippi where she grew up. His father moved out years ago. This apartment has a littered half-abandoned quality and there's an odor. Not a bad odor, but an identifying scent, like old pillows, as if windows have not been open for a long time.

But I don't care how anything looks or smells. It is an apartment in Manhattan. My boyfriend has keys to it. I have never had a boyfriend who has keys to any apartment let alone one on East 65th Street.

His sister is here today. I like it best when it is just the boyfriend and me, but he likes being around his family. Not his mother. He doesn't like her, but everyone else. He seems even proud of them. Proud of his father who smokes more than he speaks but is always recognized as the head of everything. Proud of Kitty, his Guatemalan stepmother, proud of his schizophrenic stepbrother. He doesn't seem proud so much of his sister, but he likes her company. She is not pretty-pretty. Her hair is pale and lifeless, but she bubbles like a pot of water with a big flame underneath. Like her brother, she doesn't seem burdened by dark thoughts. She seems fine. I remember how at ease she was amongst her stepmother's adult friends in the big beach house even though she does not have the looks I thought were essential for any kind of public ease.

Today the sister is packing to leave for college for the first time. We are in her room, the boyfriend cross-legged on her bed, making fun of her and laughing and she is laughing too and accepting her place as underdog, second child, the girl, unbowed by his constant teasing. It's the way they always talk to each other.

She is not wearing anything at all from the waist up. Her breasts are large. She packs, she wonders about college, she reminisces with her brother about their mother's drinking, and she moves about the room with her large breasts on full display but not mentioned.

To not mention or mind or question these large bare breasts in the room is my job right now.

After all, this sister worked at a magazine for six weeks this summer and shows us her name printed right there on the masthead. I didn't even know the word "masthead" before, but they did. She has worked at a magazine in New York City. And this new boyfriend has written a novel. I've seen that novel, a stack of typed pages. I want a stack of typed pages. I want to have worked at a magazine, but I don't know how. I don't have what they have. I don't know what that is, but I am just a girl who lives with her parents. I sure want my own apartment in a big city, but I don't know how to get that. I have nothing to show off except my prettiness and good handwriting, which the boyfriend is extolling, holding the letter I sent him last week. I like when we write letters to each other. His prose is thick, sprinkled with words I haven't heard before. It is easier to believe he loves me in the letters than in real life. "Look at this handwriting!" he is saying, holding the yellow lined sheets, while his sister moves back and forth with her bare breasts. I do not know this world where bare breasts with or without a brother is normal.

NO GOING BACK

I TRAVEL ALL DAY from my upstate school in a car full of kids to get to the boyfriend's place so we can go to a Dylan concert in his college town.

We get to the concert early and find our places on fold-up chairs in the auditorium. A girl comes by, the girlfriend he had before me, the one he tried to kill himself over. They seem to be the best of friends now, laughing and chatting. She is perfectly at ease with him and he with her. Why would he rather be with me? I can't believe that he prefers me. They seem so well suited. He will leave me one day. It will happen and I can't bear it.

The next day, as I prepare to return to my faraway school, I say we better break up. He does not say much. I cry on the train all the way back to school.

Two months go by and I am home for the Christmas break. The leaden heaviness in my chest is starting to ease as the miracle of the boyfriend and then his loss starts to fade just a bit. I knew it could not last and it didn't.

It is a dark evening, quiet, here in my family home, my parents in the living room, my littlest sister and I in the kitchen. I hear my middle sister call down from her room. My mother climbs the stairs to see what she needs. Minutes later, she comes back down into the living room. She tells us that my sister has swallowed pills and must get to the hospital as quickly as possible. Within minutes, my parents have driven away with her. My littlest sister – ten years old – comes to me in her nightgown, her small wire glasses on her nose. She lifts her arms to be held, as she begins to cry. I wrap my arms around her. Raw emotion does not well up much in this house. I didn't know I even knew how to comfort.

I help her to bed and then sit in darkness on the stairs outside her room and wonder what I should be feeling. My sister swallowing pills that she took from my father's medicine cabinet. She was the first child born after me. We seemed at odds – she assigned to my mother as I was assigned to my father. I was dark, she was blonde. She loved nature, I liked cities. I didn't pay much attention to her. We seemed to speak different languages like my mother and father did.

And now she has done this thing, interrupting the family predictability that I am so used to.

Until now, sadness and craziness have felt familiar, more natural than the joking frivolity I have seen around me in school and beyond. But now that my sister has pulled us into this world it does not feel like I thought it would. There is none of the drama of a book or a film. There is just me on these stairs, wondering what I should be feeling or saying or doing. My sister's act becomes part of everything else in this house, something to get away from.

The phone rings. It is the boy, calling out of nowhere, here in the dark. There is his familiar gravelly voice that I thought I would not hear again and it awakens every joy in me. He is sobbing. He says he wants me to come back to him. The boy is sobbing for me. He must really love me more than other people. It is easy to say yes.

I tell him about my sister because I want him to know that I am not just a suburban hick with a nice little family that sits down together every night over dinner, that I have some complexities of my own that I think he will find appealing.

I tell him too that I am starting a new school in a week. I will be moving to the city. I'll be a member of the club of city dwellers – not of such high standing as he is, but still, a walker of sidewalks, a rider of subways.

Plus, people write in cities. I know they do. Typewriters sit on desks in cities and the right words appear on the white paper in that beautiful courier font. My life will come alive in the city and the boy is back at my side.

NOT EATING

I JUST MUSTN'T EAT. That's the important thing. I don't want to eat. Or I do. I'm starving. But I mustn't. They say you should eat 2,000 calories a day. I read that in magazines. I disagree. After all, they're the same people who say I should weigh 130 lbs and if I weighed that much I'd be huge. I'm going for 100, but I can't get below 110.

I try not to eat all day until nighttime. That's what the boyfriend does, more or less. I'm in New York City and he is in his college town a couple of hours away, but I know his pattern. He sleeps until noon, but doesn't eat until he makes a big dinner in the evening, which, he is proud to say, never includes anything "green."

So, he doesn't really eat all day. When I am with him, I have to wait because I like to do what he does as if that's what I do too. Except I can never sleep till noon.

Back in New York I go to classes and just try not to eat. Sometimes, though, I break down and slide into the Chock full o'Nuts on the corner and sit at the counter and order coffee and one of their doughnuts, small and brown and crunchy with oil. It is pure heaven. But also pure hell because the night before it had seemed so easy to swear I wouldn't eat today.

Once I ate five candy bars out of a vending machine. I could not stop. At least it only happened once. The doughnuts happen more often.

In the evening, back in the dorm with its empty kitchen shared with four other girls, I pour a bowl of Grape Nuts. That is something the boyfriend sometimes eats. I have bought the Grape Nuts downstairs in the tiny supermarket. I like walking through its narrow aisles. It makes me feel like someone who lives in the city. It's like when I am with the boyfriend and we go to the grocery store and I feel independent and adult to be buying groceries. I don't say anything at all to him about it because he's used to it.

Down in the tiny supermarket, I limit myself to $5 a week. That should be enough.

I eat when: my father takes me out to dinner on Wednesdays; on weekends when I am with the boyfriend; and when my mother comes into the city now and then and takes me out to lunch. During these times I eat fiercely. By myself, which is daily life, I effort every moment to hold back the force that demands I eat.

COMFORT

I WEAR A LONG THICK BROWN COAT with a Red Riding Hood hood. The coat billows below my knees like a cape. This coat is as it should be. Especially with the brown leather boots up to my knees. The boots are uncomfortable, but I cannot buy another pair. I cannot imagine having two pairs of boots. It is richness to have one.

I live in a narrow room with a smooth gray linoleum floor, a compact yellow desk, a bookcase, a chest of drawers and a black vinyl couch that becomes a narrow bed. School furniture.

But I live in New York City.

And I have a phone. Of my own. I have never had my own phone, but the boyfriend has one so I found out how you get one and I know too that it does not have to sit on a desk. It can be on the floor. It looks so much freer down there, unusual. It is much cooler to speak with the boy on my own private phone that sits on the floor than to go out into the hall to the wall phone.

I talk with the boyfriend at night after 11 when the rates go down. If I don't talk to him I am asleep by 9. Talking on the phone after 11 is part of his world. He is up all night. His voice is gravelly, like it comes out of his throat instead of his mouth. Sometimes it is comforting to talk to him. Sometimes his "I love you's" wrap me in a quilt and for a little while nothing else gets through. Sometimes being with him is more like sharp hard things that I have to brace against, or dance lightly through as if they didn't bother me. "Aren't you jealous?" he asks after telling me he had fun talking to a pretty girl in his Philosophy class. "No," I say, "not at all." Which is not true but knee-jerk designed to keep the status quo.

"Oh," he says. "I don't know how love can exist without jealousy." As if it's okay to feel jealous and say so. That he would. But I won't.

Sometimes we fight and I slam the phone down, determined never to pick it up again and that determination lasts a day or so. But there is so much empty space where he used to be. If I take him out of my life there is not much left. I don't know why that is. He stays busy whether I am there or not. He still makes Rice Krispy chicken for dinner, he still lights up a joint, he still goes out for ice cream.

When I am happy with the boyfriend it gives me a kind of confidence. I can walk around the city as if I am a person like everyone else. I sense the bad things are still there, but if you don't look at them they are almost not there. I look somewhere else, my gaze fixed, and I go and go and go, knowing, yes, that I am walking out and out and out and that each step is on thinner substance. When will the break come, when will the boards give way beneath my feet and the world go dark?

The only good thing about the darkness, when it returns, is that it feels real and certain. I have faith in despair and hopelessness. It's the end of the road. There's nothing left to wait for. It is true and solid.

I cannot be alone though in this darkness. I reach for the boy with his gravelly voice and there are restaurants again and movies and TV and his arms around me and it fills the empty space again and I say okay, I thought I wanted something else, something more than food and movies, but this will do. The boy does not know what I mean by something else. Can't I just enjoy the movie and the ice cream? And he is right. It is so much better in his world of comfort than in mine, except —

FRENCH PHOTOGRAPHER

I WORK FOR A FRENCH PHOTOGRAPHER. The money is good. $5/hour. 8 hours/week. So when I am with the boyfriend on a weekend I have $40 in my pocket. I look rich. He doesn't know it's all I have.

I got the job from an ad on a school noticeboard. I go to her small but fancy apartment twice a week and do things like type cards for her Rolodex file. She is not the kind of hardcore photographer with a dark room and black-and-white film that I would really love. She does mostly Polaroid stuff, or if she uses regular film she gets it developed somewhere else. So I don't think it's real photography, but she's been in a book and her boyfriend is a politician who's in the papers a lot.

Her name is Marie. She's somewhere in her 40s with long old-person's dry blondish hair, a deep sort of harsh voice. She likes leather jackets and puts too much make-up on when she wants to look good. Her daughter who comes around now and then is just a year or two older than me, but glamorous and worldly and put together.

Often I am in the apartment alone. I cannot stop myself from going to her refrigerator, full of cheeses and chocolates that everybody eats when they are here. But the trouble is I can't stop. I take a little each time, trying to make it my last time. But it never is and when I leave at the end of the day I have failed again.

Marie invites me out for a weekend to her beach house in almost the same rich famous town where the boyfriend's family goes and everyone else from New York City who can. There are other people there, friends of hers. One couple sits across the table from me at lunch and talks about how they take photographs of normal things that look sexual. They look down at the roast beef sandwich on their plate, the slices of rare meat stacked thickly between bread, and look at each other with a little smile.

They are all having a wonderful time and I do my best to appear one of them, but I don't feel one of them at all. They all go out dancing in the evening. I am invited, but only half-invited, and it is easy to stay behind though part of me wishes I could just melt into their crowd, but the melting won't happen and it is more normal for me to stay in my room by myself, reading, talking to the boyfriend on the phone.

Back in the city, Marie has a new project promoting the opening of a nightclub. It has a French name. We do a bunch of publicity for weeks, sending out postcards and making phone calls, all from her living room.

And then the big opening night comes. Marie's daughter and I plus a couple of other young females will wear black shirts with the name of the club emblazoned across our chests in sparkling silver letters. I kind of dig that I am involved in this flashy unhippie enterprise.

As people bustle around Marie's apartment getting ready, I take a break to talk to the boyfriend. He is in the city in his father's new apartment for the first time. He says it's wonderful. He's all excited. It overlooks Washington Square Park, he says, and has a classy address that he is deciding how he will write – with numbers or in words. He's checked out the neighborhood – a Gray's Papaya down the block, a Häagen-Dazs across the street.

Meanwhile, everyone is getting made up. Marie's daughter, so good with these things, has said she will make me up. I can't wait. I have never worn make-up and want to see myself as a cover girl. But when she finally sits me down, she just brushes on a little mascara. I am disappointed. I had wanted to look like them, just to see if I could.

We shoot over to the new club and stand there in the lobby as people arrive. I have nothing really to do except act like I am having the best time ever. It feels like it always does with these people. Like I just cannot enter their world, or even appear to be part of it. I wish I could though, wish I could follow the crowd up the escalator and melt into the throbbing world of lights and sound. But I can't step out of myself, standing here, wearing this sparkling shirt, my feet so firmly on the floor.

SUNDAY MORNING

ON SUNDAY MORNINGS I walk down Broadway from my dorm on 119th Street to Coliseum Books on 57th, an almost-straight line. A long line, thankfully, that I walk swiftly and with purpose.

Walking is something you can do so well by yourself. It makes you feel like you have a place to go. And if you walk down Broadway on a Sunday morning it feels like anything can happen, and will, any second now. You are as far away from aloneness as is it possible to be.

I walk down to Coliseum Books and I go in and I look through the riches there, the fresh new paperbacks stacked in piles. I thumb through. I open here and there. I look at the brand new hardbacks too, but never buy one of those. Too expensive and too stiff. I go for the soft paperbacks that bend so sweetly in your hand.

Maybe I buy something.

And then it is time to return. I don't want to go back. Already I can feel the delicious surge that brought me here start to ebb.

On the walk down it was easy to feel the confidence that there is something inside me that will find its way to words on paper the moment I sit at a typewriter. If only I had a typewriter with me right now, I am sure this super-charged excitement could spill out and become something as rich as what I see at Coliseum Books.

Instead, though, it is time to return, to leave this bookstore — so worn and warm — this place where writers end up, their words — how do they do it? — neatly packaged, glowing.

I can't walk back up Broadway as fiercely as I came down. But it's still walking, it's still "on-my-way-to-writing," it's still active and in the world.

I make my way. Back to the small room in the linoleum suite — not a real apartment — I haven't figured that out yet — this narrow room with the small vinyl-topped desk at one end and the typewriter I inherited from my mother. I cannot look at it without seeing her, without seeing my whole family, the whole story of where I came from that must be erased — how can I write anything like what appears in all those piles of beautiful paperbacks when I am only who I am?

Here in the room it is impossible to be free of myself the way I was just now on the street. Here, I am the person I have always been. Out there, I was a stranger, someone who could become a writer.

CHERIE AMOUR

THE BOYFRIEND ALWAYS LIKES TO TALK about "relationships." With me, with his friends, with his sister and family. "Relationships" means, you know, with a lover. He is always confidant about whatever he says.

"My father told me at dinner," he said one night on the phone, "that he'd read that a person can have a long-term relationship with one in 40 people."

Numbers. They talk about relationships in numbers. I don't have their vocabulary. I have never thought the way they think. But the way I think doesn't fit into words as neatly as the way they think. I don't think they think in any way except in words.

He talks about monogamy. Am I for it or against, he wants to know. I know what the right answer is. I can't say I just want a safe place where he will always be nice and never think another girl might be better than me. I must not even think that. No, I must be a hitchhiker heroine, easy come, easy go.

It is warm in the city, the first days of warmth, and I go outside. I sit at the foot of a statue as crowds of students with books and conversations move back and forth across the concrete expanse of open space surrounded by heavy buildings.

I sit with a notebook. Maybe I will write something, or maybe I will just sit here and maybe someone will notice me. Someone does. He's different. With a bicycle, dark skin, overalls. No books, no conversation. Outside the crowd like me. These are always the ones who find me.

I don't talk about anything school. We talk about other things — like what the people passing by are maybe thinking about. He says he's a musician. He asks for my number and calls me in the afternoon and invites me down to his place on 14th Street.

I leave the dorm and head downtown on the subway. It's early evening. I walk through the sidewalk swarm and find his building. I enter. I climb stairs that are barren and shabby. I am in another world. It feels tricky, like I don't know what the next step will bring, but nothing alerts me directly to turn back. I knock on his door.

He lets me into a large, empty-almost room. Just a mattress on the floor. No sheets or blanket or pillow. No other furniture. I sit on the floor. He sits on the mattress. He has a guitar. He sings and strums – my cherie amour, pretty little one that I adore....

Roaches scuttle across the floor. I can see through the windows that it is getting dark and I say I will go now, and he stands up too and says he'll walk me to the subway.

As we walk side by side along 14th Street in the dark there is still plenty going on. It's like a village. Stores are open, selling cheap random stuff – toilet paper, suitcases, purses and clothes on racks. When we get to where I have to drop down into the subway we stop. He puts his arms around me and we begin to kiss. He leans me gently back against a parked car and we kiss as people swarm by, calling their kids to hurry up, lighting cigarettes, carrying bags of groceries home for dinner while radios blast music and baseball.

CLUB DINNER

I MET MY FATHER every Wednesday evening at his club for dinner. Yes, he had a club, the classy enough home-away-from-home provided by the college that he loved so much.

My father comes directly from his office wearing suit, white shirt, tie and square gold cuff links. His face is broad and square, his dark hair combed straight back from his broad high forehead. His lips are narrow, his nose straight, his eyes very blue.

He always smiles. He insists on cheer, something that looks like happiness. I claim all the disquiet behind my smile as my own.

This Wednesday date with my dad is something to go to. I don't have many things to go to apart from classes and work so I never miss.

I dress up and take my two subways that are so familiar they are almost friends, and stride across Grand Central, up the escalator and across the street, like a pro.

I meet him upstairs in the lounge bar area where he is already sitting with whiskey and soda.

I know how much he likes it here. It is his haven. He is a Hungarian immigrant tossed out on the high seas of the Second World War and he has clambered ashore. He has all the elements of a life: house, wife, children, job, and club — and probably likes the club best. Here he can sit back in a leather armchair beside a tall potted tree and a waiter will step forward to ask what he'd like.

Dad's face lights up as I enter and come towards him. "Hello, darling," he says, rolling the "r," standing with a big smile, formal, European, kissing me on both cheeks. It will be the high point of our evening. The rest is a large elaborate meal with a white tablecloth where I will eat my fill and beyond because I cannot talk. It is the only time during the week that I let myself eat freely. And while I eat my father talks his fill and beyond, the whiskey replaced by wine, having long given up on me. Once again, I have failed the conversation test.

"Thanks, Dad," I will say. Again, the kiss on each cheek and I will do my subway journey in reverse, this time without the sense of riding a wave. I will return to the small room where not enough happens. How is it that here I am in New York City, where everything is happening all the time, and yet this tiny room feels impossibly far away from where the excitement is.

PASTRY

I WALK TO THE HUNGARIAN PASTRY SHOP on a winter weekend morning. It's about 20 minutes straight down Amsterdam. I wear the boots that come to almost my knee, jeans tucked in. It is almost the look. The boots should be a bit higher and this sole that they promised would be so comfortable makes my calves ache.

It is bitter cold, but I just bite into it and march.

The Hungarian pastry shop is a destination. Not only does it have coffee and pastries, but everybody knows that people go there to write.

I am still looking for my writing. It always seems like it is waiting in the next place. When I am in the subway, I think for sure it'll be back at my desk. When I'm in my dorm room, I wonder if it would help to go to the library. Now it's the weekend and the day stretches ahead of me and I can see myself writing at the Hungarian pastry shop so that's why I'm going.

I enter the warmth of the out-of-date bakery, its tables bashed up and thrown together in a relaxed way, not many people here. I choose something with a lot of whipped cream from the brightly lit display, pour a coffee and sit at a wobbly table. With pleasure, I work my way through these completely satisfying items except they are over too soon.

I pull my notebook from the large woolen shoulder bag that goes so well with the high boots. But what do you write when you want to write? Virginia Woolf wrote Mrs. Dalloway when she sat down to write. Sylvia Plath wrote Ariel. What have I got? How do you do that? Sit down and out comes something from your deepest self and it's beautiful and it gets put in a book and people buy it in a bookstore and say you are a good writer, a real writer.

The boyfriend just sat down and wrote his novel. No big deal.

I read it recently. I didn't like it. But maybe it's good. Maybe I'm wrong. How could he have written a bad book? It's just that it's about people who aren't like me at all. People I don't even like. Maybe it would be nice to be like them, but somehow I don't believe in them. I've seen people like that in school and they never hold my interest. Life seems easy for them. They breeze along and can't imagine why anyone could have a problem. This is the kind of person the boyfriend thinks is normal.

He gave me a list of titles and said I could choose one for his book. How weird, as if a title could just be slapped on like a price tag instead of emerging out of the same mystery as the book itself. But the boyfriend does many things I would not think of.

From the list, I chose Pure Effect because that's what I thought of his writing. It's pure effect, not real writing. But I don't tell him that because he has written a novel and I haven't come close and he even has an agent. The boyfriend is so sure and right about pretty much everything and it seems like he can do so many things better than me. He is always proud of what he does while I don't feel like I have anything to bring forward, nothing ever that good to bother people with.

Here in the café, I set my pen to the paper and out come words. They look like me, splayed out there, so visible I cringe. Maybe it would be better if I were typing. It's hard to take anything in my own handwriting the least bit seriously. But I keep going. Just a little more. I am writing. It is not Mrs. Dalloway. All of that seems as far away as ever, but as I walk back up the bleak winter blocks there is something alive, heart faintly beating, in my woolen shoulder bag.

SUMMER JOB

I GET A JOB FOR THE SUMMER. It's not supposed to be just for the summer. They want full-time, forever people. It's a brand new fancy hotel, down by the United Nations. I will quit at the end of August in time for next semester, but I don't tell them that.

The hotel is so new that it isn't even open yet. They give us a tour, showing us some of the rooms, pointing out that each room contains original artwork. From the hotel I can walk to the boyfriend's old apartment, the half-abandoned one where he grew up, where no one lives anymore. But I can live there for the summer. It will be perfect!

I am to work at the front desk. They are going to train us. Things are serious. This is going to be a fancy hotel with fancy people coming and going, a place where everything has to be perfect. I've seen places like this. It's the kind of place my father would like.

I need grown-up clothes. My mother takes me to Macy's and I choose two linen suits, one white, one navy. I feel sleek and adult in them. I am going to ace this.

The boyfriend appears. He is angry. "I thought you were coming to summer school with me," he is saying though we hadn't talked about that.

He is cold and harsh. He says I have betrayed him. I am unloving for wanting to spend my summer without him. Day after day he grips me with a cruel kind of fury I have never encountered before. I am lost in this darkness, stuck in the spider web that his words weave so expertly. I have done something very wrong, he never would have done such a thing, how could I?

The long-ago night when he sobbed on the phone because I was not with him doesn't exist anymore. Nor the warm nights with ice cream, all the I Love You's and late-night phone calls are gone. I didn't know that I couldn't do something by myself. That you can't if you love someone.

He explains these things to me in bitter sentences so perfect I cannot find a gap to walk through, so high I cannot climb over or around them. My plan withers. I cannot bear his hostile heart, his dark face. I will obey, give in, send the hotel a telegram about having to move to the West Coast unexpectedly, sign up for some courses and go to the boyfriend's college for a few months. At least for the summer, my father will be able to say I attend the college of his dreams.

I have been meeting with an old hippie every week, teaching him to read. I tell him that we have to stop because the boyfriend will be in summer school and I have to go with him. The old hippie man looks at me and in his eyes I can see the weakness of my explanation. Aren't I supposed to be independent and free? I don't understand it either, but I pretend I do. After all, the boyfriend has explained it.

SUMMER SCHOOL

THE BOY IS MAKING A MOVIE. He's in a class where you write a script and then you shoot and edit the film. He wrote the script in one night. It's called Double Sixes, which is the best roll you can get when you're playing backgammon. Not that I know much about backgammon, but he does.

The movie is about a girl who plays Russian roulette, is depressed, and has sexual fantasies. He asks me to play the girl and of course I say yes. I am pretty much that girl anyway, except for the Russian roulette and sexual fantasies part, parts that would make me cooler if I had them.

There are two scenes where I have to have my shirt off with nothing on underneath. In the first one I am in bed by myself. The boyfriend is working the camera. His friend Matthew is there to help. I know this Matthew. We've all done acid together a few times. He's cute. He also goes to this fancy college. I've been to his family apartment in New York City, big and elaborate with people who are just like the ones in the boyfriend's novel.

I sit in the big double bed with my shirt off as if it is no big deal. And Matthew too acts like this is normal. It feels awful to be half naked, but that feeling is not cool so I pretend I am not even thinking about it, a familiar pretense.

The second scene I have to do without a shirt is supposed to be the girl with her shrink. The boyfriend enlisted a professor to sit opposite me while I take off my shirt and massage my naked breasts. It's supposed to be a fantasy the girl is having while she is talking to her shrink. I do this too, while looking a suit-and-tie professor in the face. I just do it. I would never admit to myself or anyone ever that I don't like doing it. I will die keeping that secret.

I have a room in a dorm. There are two other girls, but I never see them. I take writing courses and read famous books. Sometimes though I just walk into town and get a burger and milk shake. They are so delicious, everything is all right as I eat them. But I am not proud that I cannot resist these calories and that this is what I want to be doing. I should be doing great things -- writing, making art. The boyfriend spends all night editing his movie. Sometimes he comes to my room just as it's starting to get light. I wish there was something I wanted to stay up all night for.

UPTOWN/DOWNTOWN

AFTER SUMMER SCHOOL I found my own apartment back in the city. Well, not completely my own apartment. I have a small dark room, the first on the left of a passageway where other people lived, people who were older than me, people I didn't know but assumed I would, my first foothold in a NYC apartment and I thought that the address alone would bring with it friendship, camaraderie, laughter – not that such words entered my mind, just images I would never admit to wishing for.

My room did have a window but the sun never found it. The room had a tiny loft too. I had always liked lofts. The way they made two rooms out of one, so efficient. But as the months passed I never went up into this one. Too dark. Besides, I was rarely at this apartment, and when I was the old couch cushions from my high school attic room made enough of a bed.

Most of the time it was just easier to be at the boyfriend's new lavish two-bedroom, father-paid-for apartment in fashionable downtown with stereo, pot, TV, food, and him. He had finished school, spending one weekend without sleep to write his entire senior thesis. I didn't know anyone else who could have done that.

The apartment was eyesore ugly – the living room a dark salmon color with chrome and foam furniture, his bedroom walls a harsh blue. The lobby downstairs was garish with bright metallics and the elevator was staffed with men in uniform whose only job was to push the button for you. But these were the kind of things the boyfriend and his family never noticed.

Sometimes though I slammed the door on the downtown apartment, exploding in fury, striding to the uptown subway with the determination that I would never be back.

Because I know, in these moments, that life in the downtown apartment – with the color TV or the stereo going all the time – is not my place. That the things we do when I am there – watching Letterman, eating on the couch, buying ice cream at midnight – are not really my things. They are his. I do not do them when I am alone, but I know he does.

But that's the thing. What do I do when I am alone, uptown in the crunched-up room? I go for walks, I read, I walk down to the kitchen and chat for a moment with the man whose name is on the lease, but he is a stranger.

And whoever he is, the boyfriend is not a stranger. He knows me like no one.

I have noticed a new boy in a class though. Maybe he can be my new boyfriend, take the place of the old one, or be some kind of alternative. Girls in the city should move from lover to lover, right? That's what I should be doing.

I invite the new boy to walk down Broadway and stop for falafel.

He is sweet and dark-haired, brown eyes, and after dinner I ask if he wants to come over. We're just a few blocks from my place where I imagine us getting high in the living room that has – like it should – a big wooden spool for a coffee table. And then we'll sleep together. And then maybe he will fall in love with me.

Yes, says the new boy and we walk to my place. I unlock the door and step inside, but now, not even crossing the threshold, he is saying no, he cannot stay, he has to go and he is gone.

I give in. I call. The gravelly voice and words of love and regret and missing you wash over me. I get back on the familiar downtown subway.

JUST LIKE IN THE MOVIES

IN NEW YORK CITY, TWENTY YEARS OLD, not knowing that I was a young person in an old person's world, thinking I should have attained everything by now.

I have a temp job during Christmas vacation in a lawyer's office, another glitzy skyscraper office. I sit before one more Selectric typewriter stuck somewhere in the mix of receptionists and secretaries all serving the three male lawyers for whom the company is named. Boom Boom and Boom.

One of the lawyer's names is Eric. He is not handsome, but instead of wife-and-kids photos on his desk, big framed pictures of the mountains he has climbed hang on the walls. I like seeing those mountains when I go in to take dictation.

One day the lawyer with the mountains asks if I will pick up his Porsche from the garage. Yes, of course. I would like nothing more. I stretch out this errand as long as I can, driving through Central Park and finally delivering the perky little car to its reserved parking spot.

That Porsche connects us. We are outliers, rebels.

The lawyer invites me to lunch in a restaurant everyone has heard of. I only order tomato soup. "Don't you want something more?" he inquires. "The food is so good here." But I don't. It's one of those times I don't want to eat. I do drink a Margarita and he kisses me in the elevator going back up to the office.

"Don't get involved with Eric," says one of the secretaries. She's older than me, but so is everyone here. I dismiss her words. This feels like adventure, so much more exciting than everyday life.

The boyfriend has been spending every Tuesday night with Henrietta.

Henrietta is a writer. Not only that, she has published books. Not only that, she wrote the paperback that goes with the movie that is all the rage right now. And my boyfriend sleeps with her once a week. She is so old that she has an eight-year-old daughter, but she and the boyfriend have something between them that no one except them knows about. It slices me in half when I think about it, but I say it doesn't matter. I say I am okay with the Tuesday nights. Because if I say I am not okay with them, what then? Even if I could forbid it, that would not stop my boyfriend from wanting to be with someone else. He would do it without telling me.

I feel as dark as winter, but I am used to that. We are all used to that. Marta is depressed. That has been my label for years now. No one knows why. I hunt within myself to identify my weakness and correct it. My boyfriend isn't depressed. No one in his family is. They do not go out to the balcony on the 13th floor and will themselves to jump off just because their boyfriend spends one night a week in bed with a woman who is a published writer and sends him postcards sometimes.

When I go to Eric-the-lawyer's apartment for the first time I don't stay the night. I am scared to take things that far, a sixth sense that it will not be as easy for me as it has been for the boyfriend. I duck out early, saying something I heard in a movie once, "I don't like sleeping with two people in one night," and when I get home the boyfriend slams me up against the wall, his thumbs pressing on my windpipe. I can't breathe when he does that. Just like in the movies.

JUST ANOTHER PERSON

I AM ALMOST DONE WITH COLLEGE. A month or two to go.

My father invites me to lunch. As always, I look forward to the date.

My father is working in the World Trade Center these days. The selling of asphalt had not lasted long. He's been back in offices again for years.

My father suggests we meet in the restaurant at the top of one of the towers. Okay. Everything is normal so far.

Of course, I dress up. I wear the white woolen skirt that Kitty gave me. She does that. She buys so many clothes that she has to give lots of them away sometimes. The skirt flows past my knees. There's something adult and beyond my reach about it. A designer label.

I do all the things: subway then elevator. And there is my father as I have so often seen him, sitting at a table that is covered in thick white linen, sparkling glassware and heavy silver. He wears his familiar garb – suit, white shirt, gold cufflinks and tie and he is beaming. He is always beaming when you walk in.

The menu is large, my appetite is sharp and I am happy to tuck in. The city is spread out below in every direction, almost like we're in a plane.

I have not figured out how, although my family has been broke for years, my father can still manage a fancy restaurant, but I don't inquire.

Here, at the table, there isn't much in my real life I can talk about. I can't embellish on the bare facts: that I am about to finish school and drive across the country with the boyfriend to live in Los Angeles so he can be a film director; that I didn't know I was going until a few days ago when the boyfriend said I could come; that he actually said he had been waiting for me, otherwise he would have left earlier. I had had no idea, but it sounded nice. Driving across the country to go live in California sounds like fun.

My father holds his glass and relishes the view.

He signs the check with a flourish. As I move to stand up he says, "Wait just another minute. There's something I wanted to mention. You are about to finish college and, well, as you can imagine, there is a bit of a bill from the school to pay."

He is looking at me as if he is telling a joke. He has that bright laughing look in his eyes that tells you not to make a fuss, that whatever it is he is about to deliver is not such a big deal and you are silly if you think so. "Perhaps," he says, "since you will be soon be working, you would like to help pay this rather large bill."

Working? Is that what I'll be doing? I hadn't really thought about it. I mean, I've always worked, made the money I needed, but I hadn't envisioned any immediate serious change in that status. I was just looking forward to not having any more papers due.

"Okay," I say because my mind is empty of any other word.

"Very good," my father says. "That's settled then." And he gives me a kiss on each cheek and lunch is over and 30 minutes later I am back in the apartment with the boyfriend.

"He can't do that," says the boyfriend.

He can't?

No, says the boyfriend. He sees my father as just another person.

"Call him up and tell him you don't want to pay that bill," the boyfriend says. "He has no right to ask."

He doesn't? This is part of the fascinatingly different way the boyfriend sees things. He does not do things he does not want to do.

I call my father. I say, "Dad, I don't want to help pay the school bill."

"All right," says my father. His tone is even. The conversation ends right there. It did not feel natural or good, but I have taken an action I did not know even existed. It feels like stepping out of a box. I don't know if I like it out here, but there is something fresh about it, fresh and new.

PART THREE

HELLO LOS ANGELES

BEAUTIFUL, GLAMOROUS SHAYNA lives here and has already found the boyfriend a place to live, a two-room cottage surrounded by big-leaved green plants I don't know the names of. The cottage is empty except for green-and-white shag wall-to-wall carpeting and squares of mirror stuck to the bedroom wall, but the boyfriend knows to go to the Salvation Army for furniture.

He picks out a couch, a coffee table, a bed and a desk while I choose a hand mirror with a long stem and curly-cue initials on the back that I place on a short built-in shelf near the kitchen. "That," I say, "is my shelf," feeling brazen to claim any space at all here.

Then I look in the classifieds to get a job. The boyfriend doesn't need a job because his father has put him on his mail-order-jewelry company's payroll and will be sending him a weekly check so he can write screenplays and become a director. I get a job in an office that sells Yellow Pages advertising. On top of that I have to commute by city bus. I am the only person in Los Angeles who doesn't have a car and I have no idea how a person can even possibly attain such a thing. The boyfriend, of course, has the Benz, but he has to have it during the day because sometimes he has to go record-shopping or to play tennis with Lenny, the actor who lives next door.

Shayna invites us to a party. Shayna is glamorous without trying. There's just something about her that you don't want to stop looking at. Her deep voice, her dark glossy hair, her silk robes. She and the boyfriend have known each other a long time. I know he would sleep with her at the slightest come-hither, even though she is 32 and has lines at the corners of her eyes. Sometimes she sends him a card signed with a kiss of gold lipstick.

She lives in a whole house with a man even older than she is called Charles who the boy already seems to be friends with, but who to me is an unreachable stranger, utterly established in mysterious adult life. As the party winds along, a man in the kitchen asks me what I do and I have to say that I am a secretary.

If only I could say "writer" or "dancer." Even "make-up artist" would be good. My answer to the man's question is the end of the conversation as I knew it would be. It is ghastly that I am a secretary, the worst possible way to fill your days. When these people ask the boyfriend what he does he laughs, leans back, says he's here to become a film director, that he's written some screenplays, that he has some contacts. And they smile and he fits right in.

NEVER

THE WOMAN FROM THE CLINIC calls a few days later saying that the test was positive.

We have pretty much just landed in this new place, Los Angeles, and I am pregnant. I am 20 years old. I do not want at all for one second to have a baby.

I have never wanted to have a baby because I know the boy, whoever he is, this one or that one, will never stay with me if there is a baby. He will only stay as long as he thinks I am beautiful and a baby will turn me into a housewife.

I don't want to have the abortion at the clinic where it's cheapest because they use less anesthesia. I want to have the expensive abortion at the hospital where they knock you out completely.

The cost is the same as one month's rent. The boyfriend says he will split it with me.

We go on a Saturday morning. After waiting in the waiting room, I am called in. I leave the boy behind.

They put me in some kind of curtained-off place. I am lying down, waiting, when the boy bursts in. He's not supposed to be here. He is distraught and crying, saying that general anesthesia isn't safe, that I could die, that I must get up and leave right now.

I don't like that he is here, breaking the rules. The grown-ups will be here in a second and admonish him. I want just to do what I am doing, this procedure. I don't know what he is saying about anesthesia, but I have no interest. There is no way I am giving it up.

Somehow, he leaves.

In the evening, I am back home, lying on our bed. Cramps are hurting me. "Here," says the boyfriend, "maybe these will help," and he gives me a couple of Quaaludes, my favorite drug.

Soon he is kissing me and we are doing what we always do when we are in bed together.

CHICKEN OIL

THERE WAS A LARGE SQUARE CLOSET in the California cottage, almost a little room. It even had a window. Like everything in the cottage, the closet was the boyfriend's, for his stuff.

I kept my clothes there not hung up but, in recognition that I was a guest here, in the army surplus duffle bag that I had brought from New York. It stood up on its end on the floor like a tower that I dug through each morning for something to wear to work.

The days at work were meaningless, endured for the paycheck, grinding it into me that I was not writing. Each week I waited for the weekend, imagining how then I would sit and write, but even on the weekend something hijacks me.

Here it is — Saturday morning, freedom! But I am restless. The only thing I want to do is walk. The boyfriend of course still sleeps. He never gets going until noon. I leave the cottage. This is always the best part of any walk, the springing out, the certainty that the walk is alive and will take me somewhere.

And I can keep that spring going for some time, walking fast, feeling the fresh cool air of the new day. But you can't walk forever. You have to come back.

And then I am back in the cottage, the boy still sleeping, and I feel the lead weight on my shoulders. I can't pretend for one second longer that there is any possibility of anything, that I am capable of one tiny iota of what I expect of myself.

I sit down. I sit on the floor of the closet and let myself freeze into place. The boyfriend finds me.

"What are you doing?" he laughs.

"Nothing," I say. I am doing absolutely nothing, the horror of my life.

"Do something!" he says.

I don't move. I can only think of how nothing I am — a secretary only. Not a writer, after all. Nobody. Nothing. The last person in the world I would ever want to be.

The boy pushes and prods and then he goes away for a moment and comes back. Over my head I feel it and smell it, an oily mass. He is pouring the old oil that he re-uses to fry chicken. He is pouring and shaking the yellow plastic bottle over my head, its oily goo spreading into my hair, dripping onto my shoulders.

I get up. I take a shower. We get high. We go record-shopping.

PAINKILLER

THERE IS A DAY WHEN I TAKE A LETTER the boy has written to mail from the office where I work. I can run it through the Pitney Bowes machine and mail it for free. I carry the letter in its envelope to the bus stop and I smooth the white paper of the envelope so that perhaps I can read what he has written. The letter is to one of his women friends. He has many. He is good at having women friends. Women like the boyfriend. They think of him as the kind of guy you can talk to. And it's true. He loves to talk on the phone about their love life, their problems. He always has solutions.

As I walk, I smooth the envelope to see if I can read through it. I make out my name through the envelope and a few other words – "depression," "suffocating."

I feel walls closing in on me. I knew that this is what I would find if I looked through the envelope. I would find his friendship with someone else. I would find that he talks to them about me. I would find his discontent.

I arrive at this small quiet office, just a desk or two and not much to do. I think about the friend of a friend we just met who is writing a novel. I think of Lenny who lives next door and goes out to auditions. Shayna goes to people's houses and teaches them exercises. Even ordinary Wendy, another neighbor, designs clothes. Nobody goes to an office. Why do I? Because I cannot figure out how not to. I cannot figure out what others have figured out effortlessly, the creative fire does not burn bright enough in me. If it did, nothing could stop me from writing. If I had the creative force of a real artist I'd be doing it not just pining for it.

Sometimes I write here at this desk. I write on a yellow legal pad because that's what the boy writes on and he produces pages and pages. He writes with his left hand. His handwriting looks like a lot of jagged crossed sticks.

On the days when I write at the office desk I feel better. Otherwise, there's just Charlene over there answering the phone with her long painted nails and Larry, my boss, sitting in his office with the door closed. He wears a tie clip and glasses and has flat brown hair. He looks like the most boring person in the world.

I am writing a story about a man who is crazy. He pastes pictures of women on the walls of his room and they speak to him. Seductively. That's as far as I've gotten. I put the sex stuff in to make it more sophisticated, more like something the boy would write. But writing about a crazy person comes naturally.

I feel connected to crazy people, as if they know more than everyone else, something that is not what everyone else sees and talks about. They know the other things that I sense are there, but can't say anything about. Crazy people and artists. They're the ones who see the invisible and I know they are right.

But today I only think about the letter that I pushed through the mail slot in the lobby. I do not want to be who I am.

The boy is not at home today. A friend asked him to come hang lights on a film set. You see, that's what interesting people do.

I leave the office early. I cannot bear its fierce grip a moment longer. I go home. I go into the bathroom and stand in front of the sink. There is a razor blade in the medicine cabinet. The boy cut his wrists once, before I knew him. He told me about it in a letter a long time ago. He told me as if it were a secret. It felt to me like he had done something I had only thought about. He had done it, he had tried it, and years later I still have not done it though I have wanted to many times when every avenue felt closed off, always because the boy wants to be with some other girl and he says it's not important and I should not care and I say I don't but then I don't want to be alive.

I stand and cut through the skin of each wrist and look down into blue flesh I know I am not supposed to ever see. Quickly, I put band-aids on each wrist and call the boy on the film set.

And now comfort can finally come. He can say of course he loves me. He will come home and make Rice Krispy chicken and I am saved from the chasm. I can sit on the couch again next to him, my plate on my lap, watching Mork & Mindy, inhaling smoke from the blue ceramic pipe in the shape of a wizard and not think about the things that made me feel so bad this morning. I should have followed the rules. I shouldn't have read someone else's mail.

BY ACCIDENT

I AM DRIVING THE BOYFRIEND'S CAR because I am picking up my mother and little sister from a hotel in downtown Los Angeles where they have spent one night having come in by bus. They're visiting me – us – from New York for the first time and there will be luggage.

It hasn't been a good day so far. I got fired. Maybe because I cut my own hair last night in the living room without a mirror. It felt good to hack it off. The new job was almost as dead as the last one. I say "almost" just because there were people called artists involved this time. The people called artists were all a little older than me. They each had their own (windowless) space to work in, designing the little books that the company made, collections of still photos from movies with bubbles of dialog plopped where needed. Pretty bad, but still. Books. Artists. Sunset Boulevard.

My job had been just to sit still and answer the phone and feel like dying all day.

So, the boss fired me and I left. It was early afternoon and I met a co-worker in the stairwell and burst into tears and he didn't know what to make of anything. And now I have to go get my mother and my little sister.

I want to see my mother and sister, but I'm nervous. The boyfriend is unpredictable, especially with my family, or anything that is mine and not his. When my father visited a couple of months ago, I showed him our cottage in 30 seconds flat because the boyfriend was hiding in the closet. He didn't feel like seeing my dad.

How am I going to blend mother and little sister with this boy that every time I try to leave feels like such emptiness that I have to come back because at least when I am back there is a shape to things – dinner, pot, things he wants to watch, music he wants to hear. He has so many things he wants. He goes through the TV Guide with a pen as soon as it comes in the mail – comes in the mail – I mean, who does that? The TV Guide is what you're supposed to pick up at the supermarket, at the last minute, as an afterthought at the cash register. The boyfriend circles all the movies he wants to see that week, setting the Betamax to record the ones he will miss, whereas I don't care about any of it, not really – he would watch those movies even if I wasn't here. If he wasn't here, I wouldn't have a TV.

But what would I do instead? That's the trouble. That's where I get stuck.

And now my mother and my little sister are coming into the middle of all this. It is afternoon and the air and haze of L.A. are happy to choke me as they almost always are. I am in back-to-back traffic in that tiny chunk of L.A. called "downtown" that pretends to be a city and the boyfriend's big old inherited Mercedes is roaring and pushing forward as if my foot was pressing the gas pedal to the floor, but I'm not. Instead, I am practically standing on the brake with both feet, pressing as hard as I can because the car wants to burst forward into the car inches ahead of me.

A parking garage on my right offers escape. I pull into it, but am immediately on a downward slope, the extra incline adding enough momentum to make this a now completely runaway car. A cement wall looms and I give up. I say, okay, let it happen, this is going to kill me, something really awful is going to happen now and I am going to let it.

The car smashes into the cement except it isn't cement. It's something you can smash right through. We go right through the wood, the plaster, whatever it is. And then we stop.

RENDEZVOUS

I'VE BEEN IN L.A. FOR LONG ENOUGH now that when I need a job I look at Variety and The Hollywood Reporter, in that order.

They both come out every day, both on shiny white paper. Variety writes its name across the top in bright green, The Hollywood Reporter in red.

I have a car now. This is a miracle. Shayna gave me her old one. It is a white and orange Pinto and they say if you get rear-ended the car can explode. I don't care about this and I don't care that I have to put oil in it every few days. I have learned to buy oil at the supermarket where it is cheaper and I've learned to read a dipstick.

It's always hot and stifling in Los Angeles. There is too much cement here. Car cement, which is different than New York sidewalk cement. I miss New York, which is a city. L.A. is one big suburb with palm trees.

I just got another job on Sunset Boulevard. I'm the secretary for a literary agent except it's not books. It's pilots and screenplays. I like when I know some of the names that roll across the screen in the evenings when the boyfriend and I are watching what he wants to watch. I smoke the pipe with him and sometimes I go to the bedroom to read, but then I always fall asleep even though I try hard not to. The boyfriend taunts me when he walks through.

I drive Nancy to work in the mornings. She is past 25, almost a different generation. I see lines at her eyes. She smokes cigarettes and lives with Lenny, the cute black actor, a few cottages down from us. She is very pretty, very blonde with the blue eyes. She is not a hippie. She wears a white nurse's uniform for work and takes her furniture seriously. One morning as I am leaving the cottage to join her as she waits for me outside, we hear smashing glass coming from inside my home. "We're fighting," I say to Nancy, and she understands. Lenny sometimes starts screaming, thinking she is having an affair with a doctor at work, the last thing Nancy will ever do.

"There's a new book that says eating sugar causes depression," says the boyfriend one day. He's found it out from Kitty, the family expert on everything mood-altering. So I have to stop eating sugar. It seems ludicrous that a random food could cause how I feel. But if I don't try it, it'll seem like I like feeling this way.

I begin to read food labels and find sugar in things that aren't even sweet. It becomes a hell trying to never ever touch a drop of it. I begin to stop at the supermarket on the way to work to buy Fritos just to take my mind off the coffee cake that will come through on a trolley at 10 am, just when you need it most.

I have already tried anti-depressants. The boyfriend suggested them too, via Kitty. She was all into them. It didn't seem right to me that a pill could take away my feeling. Even though I hated feeling depressed, it felt real. It felt like me. But I was curious. Perhaps I really could never feel bad again.

The anti-depressive doctor was an old man in a small office. I sat beside his desk and without much conversation he tossed off a prescription. I took the pills. I didn't notice any difference. I went back to him. He told me to double the prescription and I quit. I didn't trust him, his methods or his pills.

And now the boyfriend is going back to New York for a month. His father is laid up from a taxi accident, and the boyfriend wants to keep him company. Okay. The night before he is to leave, we go out for dinner to our favorite Chinese restaurant. We order our favorites: chicken with peanuts and mu-shu pork. We eat with appetite and relish. But this is what is different. I am talking. I am laughing. I suddenly have an abundance of entertaining things I want to tell the boyfriend about. He is laughing. I have come alive. It feels so good. I don't know where it came from, but I am reveling in this lightness that is usually so out of reach.

"You get happy just as I'm leaving," the boyfriend says, but I laugh it off. I don't care why I am happy. I am just so grateful for the relief.

A few days later he calls from a Manhattan coffee shop, saying he can't stay on the phone long because he's meeting a girl. Someone he just met on the subway.

My insides turn to stone. I imagine him on the subway, striking up a conversation with a girl who he thinks is pretty, a girl who is like him. I imagine her not stunning, but cute, on his wavelength, that one I'm not on.

I dress up much sexier for Halloween than usual — leotard, tights, tall gold heels. There's a party or two, but despite the outfit I connect with no one. Just before giving up for the night, I drive to Ralph's, the 24-hour supermarket, and walk through the aisles with a cart, picking up one or two things, but looking for someone to find me. No one does.

Eric, the New York lawyer I never quite slept with, calls. He's done that once or twice since I came to California. This time he asks if I'd like to meet him in the Virgin Islands for the weekend. His timing is good. I let the boyfriend know and catch my plane. I bring along manuscripts from the slush pile at work. It feels good to be a grown-up bringing manuscripts to read.

It is fancy in the Virgin Islands. There are three or four other lawyers with Eric. They meet together in the mornings while I drive Eric's rented convertible around the island. In the evening we take a boat to a tiny island that only has a restaurant on it, nothing else. And I feel pretty amongst the other men. I can hold their attention. But Eric doesn't love me. I feel it quickly and by Sunday I hardly say goodbye when we part at the airport.

Back at work on Monday, Jenn, the sweet young receptionist, is holding the phone, covering it with her palm. "It's your boyfriend," she whispers, her eyes wide. "You better hold onto him, Marta. He's the real thing."

I take the call, sitting on the black leather couch in my boss's empty office. The boyfriend, still on the East Coast, is sobbing and desperate, saying how much he loves me, how much he misses me. We don't mention my weekend away.

BREAK AWAY

I SLAM THE DOOR.

It's the middle of the night.

I storm to my car, parked on the street. I know where I'm going. I saw a sign last week. Apartments for rent. I'm going there.

It's too early for anyone to be up. I park near the building that has the sign, lock my car from the inside, put the seat back as far as it will go and sleep. He has no idea where I am.

In the morning, I go to the door of the building. It is on a sloping street. The Hollywood sign overlooks us.

An old woman comes to the door. She has a cigarette in her hand, is dressed in a bathrobe, and has thin dyed-red hair. She says her name is Rose and she takes me up one set of carpeted stairs to show me the apartment she's renting.

I make the deal. I have my own place.

The bed comes out of the wall and folds back up into it. There's a couch in the living room. The kitchen has a built-in bench and table. The bathroom is painted a happy robin's-egg blue. I can be here alone, by myself. I like it.

What are the boyfriend and I now? Broken up? Yes, sort of. But he is still there, in the background.

I do things. I go to the art museum. I go to many little ones and look at paintings made by people who are also living in Los Angeles.

I look for new friends. I have dinners out with other women. I start to eat organic vegetables and go to yoga classes. I visit a boy in the next apartment one night because maybe we will like each other. But after sex I come right back home and don't want to see him again. Nor he me.

I am an editor now at a paperback publishing company where I started out as secretary to the editor-in-chief, Pat, who is the best boss on the entire planet — short, plump, middle-aged, Irish, gay. Pat never talks office-ese. Everybody loves him.

I write the copy for the back covers of paperbacks and even now and then get to choose a manuscript for publication. I have my own office and a business card. When Pat needs a screenplay adaptation written over a week-end I suggest the boyfriend who writes the book in two days and makes $1,500.

"Why don't you send Pat a thank-you card?" I suggest to the boy. I mean, the whole thing has been a bit of a miracle.

A few days later Pat shows me what the boy sent, a postcard depicting a line of construction workers up high on scaffolding overlooking Manhattan, all of them pointing their naked butts to the camera. This is not what I had meant. I am embarrassed by the boy. Pat doesn't seem to care. So maybe what the boy sent is okay.

ATTEMPT

"YOU HAVE NO AMBITION," my father said. "You are like your mother."

We were on Sunset Boulevard. He was driving. We were in a rental car because he was visiting. It was dark and we were returning from a day's drive up the coast. It was the end of our weekend together and I was ready for him to leave. There had been a lot of hope in the anticipation of this visit.

He had come because I had written him a letter in which I had attempted to break what felt like a lifelong silence. Sending that letter had felt as daring and frightening as jumping off a cliff, saying things I had never said before, wanting my father to see me in a way he had never done before.

"I have a business meeting in Texas," my father had written in response. "I will extend my trip to come see you and then we can talk about your letter."

He knocked on the door of my new second-story apartment and I let him in. At least this time there was no boyfriend hiding in the closet. He said he had arrived in town that afternoon, had rented a car and had already explored the territory and chosen where he'd take me to dinner. "It's something I can always do in any city," he said, leaning back on the couch that I had upgraded with a white bedspread. "My inner homing device can always find the best restaurant."

I lit a joint and offered him a hit. After all, this was about being truthful. I wanted him to see my life, what I really did, who I really was.

He wrinkled his nose, declining with distaste.

The restaurant he had chosen was high up, poised in the darkness above the wide blanket of the lights of Los Angeles. It had all the elegance my father enjoyed and that I expected when I was with him.

We played the graceful couple, side by side, taking our seats, murmuring to the waiter, taking the luxury of white linen and heavy silver for granted.

It was like the old days. My father talked, me contributing little. There wasn't much room for my tiny life, my little job as an editor at a paperback publishing company, my attempt at independence in the new apartment. But my father had room to be expansive, leaning back with his whiskey and soda and telling me how the business contacts in Texas were enthusiastic about a program called EST that was supposed to change your life and how, to placate them, he had taken part in a seminar but had written a false name on his nametag. As always, he wanted me to know that he had outwitted the opposition.

During dessert I said what had been building in my brain. "So, Dad, shall we talk about my letter?"

"Oh," he said, "we can do that tomorrow."

The following day he wanted to drive up the coast. "My letter?" I asked as we drove.

"A little later," he said. "Let's just enjoy this beautiful drive."

He didn't want to talk about the letter during lunch either. I felt like a horse that wanted to gallop being made to wait in the stable. As he talked, my mind had long ago fallen into its familiar rut of full but silent revolt.

Finally, we sat out on the sand by the waves, and he said that now was the time. I didn't know how you talked about these things, but I was sure we had to. And what were the things? Well, mostly I had felt that there had been no honesty all those years at home, no one really talking about what was true. But how do you talk about what is true?

"Early on in life," my father said at one point, "I realized I was not good at relationships and I decided to focus on my work instead." I knew that wasn't the right answer. What the right answer was I could not figure out. I had hoped that by just puncturing the silence I might get somewhere. But the road ahead seemed just as unlit.

We stood, brushed the sand from our pants, and drove back to Los Angeles.

ONWARD

AND NOW THE PUBLISHING OFFICE is moving to New York and they have said I can come too, and I am overjoyed. They will even pay for my ticket. I'll leave in January. I've been in L.A. for three years.

It is Christmastime, a few weeks before I am to leave. The boy and his family are meeting up in Mexico and he invites me to come along, like in the old days.

We stay in a place that is all open terraces, shaded by vines and flowers, overlooking the sea. No other guests. Each day we come together for sumptuous meals outdoors. It is Kitty and the father, the boyfriend, his siblings — full, half and step — and the usual assortment of Kitty's friends, one of whom is an older woman. I haven't met her before, but I know who she is. I know that the boyfriend slept with her once, not too long ago. He went over to her apartment, she opened the door, and they went to bed together.

Seeing her here at the table slices into me. She is on the boat when we waterski. She is not beautiful. She is not anything. Except someone the boyfriend went to bed with and I cannot bear it.

Days go by. We are in paradise, they say. "Don't be unhappy," says Kitty, laughing and shoving a chunk of hash into my mouth on New Year's Eve.

Back in Los Angeles, the boy calls me at work. I shouldn't move to New York, he is saying, his voice gritty and deep. I shouldn't because because because. He has reasons lined up like soldiers who never miss their mark.

I am reduced to tears, there in the office, but I won't let go of New York. I cannot give this up. I have been wanting New York since I met Los Angeles. Los Angeles has never been my place. I say goodbye to the boyfriend on his porch after one more night together. His sister drives me to the airport. Am I leaving the boy? Or just going away? We don't know. But I can't wait to return to the sidewalks, to the grit and the compact world that again promises a writing life. I'm 23.

PART FOUR

NO INVITATION

I DID NOT INVITE MY FATHER to the wedding. Well, it was impossible for him to come, I reasoned. Too expensive to fly in from Hungary. I did not invite him. Hardly mentioned it. Wasn't talking to him much in those days. Though he had come to visit the previous year and Fred, my soon-to-be husband, this writer whom I had fallen in love with hard – had met him.

The three of us had spent an afternoon together – not in Fred's and my Woodstock home. No, Fred and I had gone down to see my father while he was visiting my mother where she was living an hour away. My father had been back in Hungary for a good 15 years by then. And my mother had divorced him though that really hadn't changed anything. In fact, the divorce seemed to have dissolved the recriminations of the past into some kind of friendship. My mother could not stop taking care of him. He could not help needing her and maybe even, just very slightly, appreciating her.

The four of us had had a cup of something together and then Fred and I had taken my father out to lunch. But we kept it simple. Sandwiches from a deli, sitting at a picnic table in a park. I'd never seen my father order a sandwich in a Catskills deli before, a far cry from the world of white tablecloths. But Fred and I had no money and I had wanted to keep things very very real.

Afterwards Fred had said, "Your father was riveted on you the whole time." I had not noticed.

I did not invite my father to my wedding. I was trying to create a new life where I didn't follow my old patterns, especially the family ones. Being with Fred had given me a taste of a new freedom and possibility. I don't know. It's hard to explain. But I didn't invite my father to my wedding.

FATHER IN BUDAPEST

THERE HIS BOOK SITS.

In plastic wrap. Brand new. Unopened. Displayed on a small table not large enough for anything else.

My father has created this room. It is him. He lives now in the Budapest apartment his grandparents bought when he was four years old. My father has come back to Hungary to live, though he does not emphasize the seeming permanence of this move. Once, I heard him say that he was not exactly living in Budapest, but commuting back and forth to the States. My eyes had rolled and my soul had coiled into a fist. "Oh, for fuck's sake, Dad. You are living in Budapest because you can't make money in the States anymore, because you went bankrupt, sold the house and could not recover and in Budapest you can live pretty nicely on your Social fucking Security. Could you please just say that?" I did not say that.

I am visiting him here in Budapest in this high-ceilinged, pre-World War I apartment where I remember my grandparents living, and my great aunt, and my aunt with her jovial husband. I remember being a kid here and eating with Hungarian relatives around a rectangular table with a tablecloth, yellow soup in a tureen, a large chicken claw floating in the otherwise clear broth.

Now the room, decades later, is my father's study, the book he wrote and published when I was in high school displayed by the window, a large heavy desk worthy of a statesman in one corner, long dark red brocade or damask drapes hanging at the window overlooking the street. I used to stand at that window, 12 years old, and watch every movement of every person and tram passing by below, wishing I could be down there, an adult in a city.

My father has chosen everything in this room. The heavy armchairs upholstered in pale silk, the over-sized polished wardrobe. He has created this room in which to meet his public; it is the place where he can best play his part. He tells me how he could buy these impressive pieces of furniture because they came from estate sales.

It is not like him to discuss a bargain. In fact, he has never stooped to the distasteful task of economizing. The father I know prefers to wave wands and make money come out of nowhere, no questions asked.

In the small kitchen where my grandmother used to cook he pulls a slim glass from a cupboard and flicks it with a fingernail. "Hear that?" he asks. "That's how you know it's real crystal."

But I have just come from the airport and I don't give a flying fuck about crystal. I am famished and tired in that awful international-flight way, and he has no food because he thought it would be better, he says, to go to the supermarket together so I could choose what I wanted.

But I am afraid as we go up and down the aisles, afraid to spend his money. I imagine there is very little. "Would you like this?" he asks, pointing to cheese or chocolate or cookies and I am too confused. It's hard to to say yes to anything beyond essentials.

And then, as we go through the cashier, he drops the eggs, all of them, a gooey mess at his feet. A flurry of women assure him it's nothing as they mop up the mess while he stands to the side – polite, apologetic, but accepting their ministrations as his due.

DISTRICT VIII

ACCORDING TO HUNGARIAN LAW, if your father was Hungarian then, no matter where in the world you were born, you are Hungarian too. All you have to do is prove that your father was Hungarian. Well, I thought, I can do that.

Of course, the authorities don't make it easy. I tracked down the documents needed, but one eluded me: my father's birth certificate, and it was proving impossible to find.

I had asked my aunt in what district of Budapest my father had been born, knowing you needed that detail to locate a Hungarian birth certificate.

"XII," she had answered without hesitation, which made sense. The family apartment – our hub for almost 100 years – is in District XII.

But District XII had no record of my father's birth. Thinking the birth certificate must have been destroyed in the war, I started to gather corroborating evidence of his birthplace in the hopes of making a convincing argument – the hand-drawn family tree, for instance, which took his family line back to the 1600s, every one of them, on both sides, born in Hungary.

One night as I was getting into bed, I thought to take a look at the manuscript of my father's autobiography. Maybe I could include it with my application. I flipped open the cover, thinking I'd do a quick skim. My eyes, however, went to the very first sentence and there it was: "I was born in Barsonyi clinic, on Ulloi Street in District VIII."

District VIII! He had put the crucial missing piece in the very first sentence where I'd be sure to find it.

Within 24 hours I had his birth certificate and all sorts of new thoughts about Dad – how that now he was dead, maybe we could be the good friends we were meant to be, how he had left me that clue all those decades ago that would surface just when I needed it, and I even took to asking his help, thinking I had an ally out there in the spirit world.

And then on Thursday, in a session with a therapist, she asked me, "Is there a relationship in your past where your importance was secondary?"

And there he was again: Suspect #1, Dad.

And I saw myself in my mind's eye, walking towards him through the small living room. I am a teenager. He is in the front hall that serves as his bedroom at night. He is wearing a suit and tie and he is scooping change out of a bowl on a low dresser and putting it in the left pocket of his suit jacket. We are going out. I have dressed up. He looks at me. His eyes approve.

But he is the one in the position to approve. And I am the one whose job it is to be approved of. It is the natural order of things, unquestioned, except by me, on Thursday, sitting in my car, parked, holding my phone in my hand, looking at its screen, at my therapist's face and remembering that in the beginning my favorite person thought of me as less important than himself.

FOLDED COAT

WHAT IS THIS? AM I GOING SOFT? I have been missing my father. Missing what he'd be saying if he were with me on my walk this afternoon because of course he would be the one talking and I would be quiet. He would have an endless stream of words coming out of his mouth, words that suffocated me, but his conversation has finally been stilled.

This afternoon getting into the car to come home I took off my coat, the kind of coat you wore with dresses when I was little, a coat with buttons and a shiny lining, and I folded it the way my father had taught me to fold a coat so that the lining was on the outside. "This way the coat stays clean," my father had told me and I thought until recently that this was a common law, something everybody was taught, but nobody folds a coat like he taught me to, and when I do it, or when I don't, I think of him, and this afternoon it felt like doing homage. "Here, Dad," I thought, placing my folded coat in the back seat, "this one's for you."

Is this piece that is surfacing, this piece about missing him, is it just one facet of the multiple facets of how I feel about him, all the stories I have told about him, the stories that sit in the special stack of notebooks on the bookshelves, waiting to be typed and collected and put together? Will it be a dark collection with now and then this odd little glimmer of after all, I miss him?

It is easier to miss him knowing that he will never enter the room again.

I don't know what story I am writing, but I will keep the story of my father and me, and I will keep writing it down, because it's a story I want to tell. I want people to know how little I once was, and how big he was, how he defined our world at home, at least the part I liked best – at least at first — how I wanted to be like I thought he was — the center of attention, good at things that were worth being good at like having others turn their faces toward him as if to the sun, and how he lost his shine as I got older, lost his shine but not his power so that where once I was happy to look up and smile at him no matter what, the smiles became grudges and fury so clad in fear that it could not be spoken.

And on through decades of living by his values and landing on my face, on my knees, and having to find instead something else that worked — nothing close to what he had proposed — so that by the end I gave up on him. I did not call. I let him die because I had no trust that any word he said would be a real word.

MY HUNGARY

SEVERAL YEARS AFTER my father's death, it came over me that I wanted to formally study Hungarian, my father's language.

Hungarian – the language, the country, the culture – has been a member of our family since my earliest memories. My father spoke with pride of his country, he sang Hungarian songs with gusto, beating time with his thick gold wedding band against the roof of the car as he drove, window open. My sisters and I sang with him, parroting the words, not knowing what we were singing about but singing with equal gusto. We used a few basic Hungarian words and phrases around the house, letters came on blue tissue paper from relatives in Budapest. Hungary was just a natural part of home, our personal country, a place that in the beginning I thought only we knew about.

After several childhood visits, I found myself visiting Hungary about once every ten years on my own and making scattered attempts to learn the language here and there without much satisfying progress.

But suddenly, a few years ago – in the midst of a full-time job, writing, and keeping up with home life, I wanted to learn Hungarian. And I wanted to go to Budapest again. It took me by surprise, these desires so strong I had a ticket booked within days and a Hungarian teacher calling me every Tuesday at noon.

I had thought that once Dad was gone my tie to Hungary would be over too. But now it didn't feel that way. I had thought it was just his place, but as I crept my way back into the language – and even the place itself – Hungary, I saw, was so embedded in my earliest memories that it was just as much mine as his. Just as a childhood toy can reconnect you to that faraway time of infancy, so Hungary and the sound of Hungarian tied me back to my most original days.

"Your accent is almost perfect," said my teacher, thrilling me. I had known the sound of Hungarian since baby years. I didn't know its grammar or much of its vocabulary, but I knew its taste and rhythm, the only part no one can teach you.

And always, as I studied, I thought of my father. I understood for the first time that he had been a native of this language, not just a person who spoke English with an accent. Before his English-speaking life he had been part of this country and this culture as much as anyone else there, something so obvious but not visible to me before.

SMALL TALK

WHEN I WAS IN BUDAPEST this summer I did not go see my father's grave. I had thought I might.

I made sure I saw Beethoven's piano in the museum, but not my father's grave.

Yesterday in Hungarian class, Zsuzsa, my teacher, was introducing all the phrases to do with weather. It's raining. It's snowing. It's windy. She then added that in Hungary people do not talk about the weather. It is considered trite, not worthy of conversation. She went on to say that she had lived in England for many years and had noticed that people there speak freely about the weather, and how she had come to realize that this kind of idle chit-chat with strangers served a purpose. She had even warmed to it despite her upbringing.

Her words swung open a door for me. "Oh, Zsuzsa," I said. "I have to tell you something!"

We were in the big gray car. I was about 11. My father had invited me to come with him as he drove some guests to the train station to find their way back to London after visiting us for the afternoon. On the way to the station the woman said to my father, "Miklos, you always live in places with nice names. Do you choose where to live based on the name?" She was laughing. It was a joke.

On the way home, the guests now on their train, my father was scornful. "Living some place because of its name. Did you hear her? She was making small talk, and small talk is the lowest form of conversation." These words were not delivered casually. They were entered into the etheric manual my father had been putting together for me since Day One on how to live correctly and be better than other people.

Back in the present, my teacher understood. "If Hungarians are stuck in an elevator," she said, "they are uncomfortable speaking with others to pass the time. They will remain silent and uncomfortable rather than chat about empty subjects."

It was a revelation that my father's long-ago denouncement of chit-chat was actually something he'd absorbed from his culture, a culture created not by diverse groups of people, but by one unadulterated tribe.

I have always known my father was Hungarian. Until recently, it sounded like a label without consequences. But I am learning it is much more than a label. It is definitive in many ways. Growing up in Hungary at a particular time in history painted my father a particular hue, a hue that blended imperceptibly with his personality until the two could not be told apart.

DON'T CRY

MY HUNGARIAN AUNT is younger than my Canadian mother, but she sounds older and when you ask her how she is she says in her accented English simply, "I am old," as if her next step is into the grave. She is the one I will visit in August though I will not stay with her. I will stay just down the street in a studio apartment, about $50 a night, a small miracle to have found just what I was looking for in the city of Budapest.

But I will sit in my aunt's apartment again, the apartment I have known since childhood, a place that will bring me close to my father, as close as anything on earth can. I may go to his gravesite. I have never been. But I don't expect to feel his presence there.

But I will feel it as I walk up the dirty marble stairs that curve to the left, my footsteps echoing with a hollow sound, the stairs my great grandparents climbed. The ones he climbed as a child and for the last 25 years of his life. I will go as far as the first floor where the stairs open onto the outdoor corridor that overlooks a neglected courtyard of patchy grass. I will walk along the railing, passing the two or three other front doors on my left, until I come to the last apartment. Here is where my relatives stand and wave when you arrive and when you depart. My grandparents did it, my great aunt. My aunt did it and her husband. My father did it. My great grandparents must have done it too.

This apartment has cast a spell on me. It is the only place from childhood that I can return to. The cluster of people I call my family has lived here for almost 100 years. But it won't last. When my aunt dies her goddaughter will inherit.

I wish I could keep this apartment, but maybe then it would not feel

so precious. It would become a practical burden. When I go in August I
imagine I will sit within its walls, absorb it, maybe I will photograph it, but
some things you just can't capture.

We visited twice in the '60s when I was 11 and 12. I think often these
days of the grown-ups of those visits: my grandparents, my great aunt, my
aunt and her husband, five people living in what roughly translates as a
three-bedroom apartment. I think of my trim pretty grandmother during
our visits, parsing out the money so that everyone got fed, thinking up
things to do with the children – us – walks in the park, an ice cream, a visit
to a famous church.

My grandfather, who spoke not a word of English, sat alone in the
afternoons in a small room by himself. He wasn't reading. Just sitting. He
wore an old suit that hung loosely. When he came with us to the park he
walked slowly with a cane. His face was wide but not fat, his expression
sour, the lines of his face engraved deeply into his skin, pulling his expression down. Despite his scowl, I was not afraid of him. But he was unreachable in his Hungarianness, his oldness, his lack of laughter though I sensed
he had softness somewhere.

When my father bade him goodbye at the close of one of those childhood visits – in the room where until the day before a table had been set up
for big lunches and where my sisters and I had slept – my grandfather begins
to sob, tears running into the grooves of his face, over the stubble on his
chin, as he sits, his hands grasping the cane that pokes up between his knees
while my father stands over him, one hand on his shoulder, saying concilia-
tory words in Hungarian. From my father's tone, I know he is saying things
like, don't worry, we'll be back, don't cry, words I can see have no effect,
and yet he keeps saying them.

STATIONERY

I BOUGHT THIS SMALL NOTEBOOK in a modest Mom-and-Pop stationery shop on Böszörményi Út, the family street, in Budapest this summer. I had prided myself on being able to read the identifying sign as I
passed by and was curious to see what kind of lovely notebooks I might
find. It was a sorry little stationery store and I bought this notebook mostly
not to hurt the proprietor's feelings. I can always make use of another easy-
to-carry notebook.

The little stationery store was at the far end of our short street, just before the juncture with the large avenue that led to the big subway and train
station. I passed the little store often.

In boarding school, aged nine, we had to sit at our desks on Sunday
mornings and write letters. Other girls had letter-writing kits, some quite
elaborate – zippered leather folders with compartments for pen, notepaper,
envelopes and stamps. New to British boarding school culture, I just had a
box of envelopes and a pad of writing paper my mother had left me with.

We sat silently at our desks, some nun sitting up front, reading the Bible
to herself, or a missal, or maybe saying her rosary, keeping order just by her
presence.

You had to fill the time. After writing to my family – one letter to cover mother, father, and both little sisters – I began dipping into the barrel of
relatives none of whom I knew very well, none of whom I had exchanged
letters with before. But now I wrote to them, and sometimes they wrote
back, which was like winning the lottery, to have a letter arrive with your
name on it.

That's when I started writing to my Hungarian grandparents and the others of the apartment. I learned where to put the dots over what letters as I wrote out the address the Hungarian way: city first, then the street.

My father returned to this apartment to live after 30 years in the States. He died in the apartment, in his sleep. Everyone died in the apartment. Only my aunt is left, in her 80s, living with a woman who cooks and cleans and keeps things going.

Márta Néni, my aunt and namesake, was always the vigorous one. She had tremendous physical energy. Now her hair is white and unbrushed. She doesn't take much care with her dress. Her face is sad. "I am old," she says again.

This summer I took pleasure in being within the embrace of the apartment again. The kitchen is small now, a three-person table pushed up against the wall, the sink tiny. It had seemed large when I was little, full of women, the source of a flow of food that came out without effort it seemed to a large table with a white cloth. Decades later, when my father lived there, he used that same front room as his office where he received visitors.

Now my aunt sleeps in this room. My father's heavy desk, the bookcases and drapes are gone, replaced by light ordinary furniture. I see his two silk-covered armchairs pushed into the adjacent room where my grandparents used to sleep, a room that seems now to serve no purpose, unheard of in years past when every inch was needed.

I can't take photos of the apartment as one friend suggested. I can only take photos of the people living there — my aunt and Shari who takes care of her — with the apartment as the setting. That's when you can really see it or feel it, its age and character. Without a face or two, it appears almost shabby. Perhaps we have used it up. Perhaps it needs a new family.

LAST VISIT

I SHOULD HAVE GONE TO SEE HIM. I used to drive to work, knowing he was old and sick, and asking myself over and over if I would regret not going. I knew the generic advice: of course you go to see your father, you have to go. Not for any reason. Just because it's the right thing to do. But I didn't trust popular wisdom. I wanted some tangible reason of my own, a motivation, and though I searched I couldn't find it.

So I did not go because I was certain, and I still am certain, that I would have simply found my father as he had always been so what was the point?

Tonight though, I can imagine going, not for something new to happen but just to say goodbye, to look at him one last time, thinking there he is, this man who defined and dominated, here we are in our last chapter.

So if I had the choice tonight I would go, just to kind of put a period at the end of the sentence, not that the sentence will ever end.

The last time I saw him I was as sure as you can be that this was the last time. He was in the front seat of an expensive taxi that he could not afford, Fred and me in the back.

My father had insisted on calling a cab and going in style back with us to the apartment where we were no longer staying on the other side of the Danube. Fred and I were on a two-week visit and my father did not know that we had just switched apartments, that in fact we were now staying just a few blocks from his own apartment. I had not told him, fearful that our proximity would open the door to greater interference. He had already tried to come on our three-day trip through the country. I'd only avoided that by leaving a day early.

Now it was the last night of our visit. Our plane would leave tomorrow, and true to celebrational form my father wanted to take us home by taxi. I tried to talk him out of it; I didn't want him to spend the money on a trip that was not necessary. Fred and I could walk to where we were staying. But my subterfuge had painted me into a corner. My father insisted. I submitted, knowing Fred and I would just have to turn around and come back on the subway.

My father directed the driver to take us slowly past the castle lit up at night. He wanted to treat us like royalty. He wanted to treat himself like royalty. To hell with money that he didn't have and we didn't either for the sake of a sweeping, leisurely view of the lit-up castle at night on a broad boulevard. He spoke as we drove of history — the castle's, his own. He had lived in this city until his early 20s when he slipped out, escaping the Communism that came after the war.

The taxi pulls up at the apartment we were staying in last week.

"Goodbye, Dad," I say, "thank you," and I lean forward as he turns from the front to kiss me on each cheek. I know there will be tears in his eyes and there are. We both know that the chances of seeing each other again are unlikely.

But we can make nothing further of the moment. There is only goodnight to be said. Goodnight, thank you, goodnight, thank you, sweet dreams.

TIME TRAVEL

I CALLED THE BOYFRIEND from the car.

I was near the end of a long drive down to the fancy part of Long Island, the part I only got to know at all because 45 years ago his people had a house there, on the ocean, countless rooms, house guests, ocean front, the whole nine yards.

I hadn't been back since, but a chance encounter was bringing me into that tony neighborhood again.

Why was I calling the boy? To see if he really would be there after all these decades, living behind the phone number from 45 years ago, in the same apartment where we'd been teenagers together. Was he living at all?

The thought of dialing that number that I had never needed to write down had often tempted. It would be like dialing back in time. Hard to resist. Sometimes I'd go for months without thinking of him. Then he'd be back in my head for days. The last time we'd spoken was about 12 years ago when I'd hung up on him after three minutes.

It was 11:30 in the morning when I called from the car. Dicey whether he'd be up. On came the answering machine with his snarky voice that when I was 18 had sounded so daring. "Don't leave a message," it said. "I never check this machine." So I didn't.

20 minutes later I have scrambled down a sidewalk in the pouring rain and found a little lunch place. That's when the phone rang. His number. I turned it off. Not here. Not when I'm having lunch. And now the idea of talking to him was getting a little more constructed — not the spontaneous call from the highway, a little more scary.

But when lunch was done and I was back in the parked car — rain streaming down the windows, I called back and he picked up.

The thing is to stay with myself, always. Not a word will I say, nor a breath will I take during this conversation that does not come from my anchored self. That is the promise I make. It's the only way to attempt this, and it's a risk.

I do easy things. I ask about his family and hear about people who a long time ago seemed like important parts of my own life, but really they were people he thought were important and I was along for the ride, clinging because without his world I thought I had nothing at all.

After some updates that slip by me unnoticed I ask, "Are you still writing?"

No, no, he'd given that up a long time ago, he says. No future in it.

No future in it?

Oh. I hadn't known that about him. Back then, when we were kids, I had thought he was writing for the same reasons I was.

It's when he talks about his niece that I finally get it.

I have never met this niece, yet he starts telling me how happy the family is because she's finally "in a relationship," how they'd been so concerned for her all these years because she wasn't "in a relationship."

It was the way he talked about "relationship." Exactly as he used to when we were 20. Just hearing him say the word brought back what felt like an ancient culture, his focus and interest in "relationship," the kind you read about, the kind experts tell you about, the kind that exists in your mind devoid of experience. Implicit in the boyfriend's tone, as always, is his expertise on the subject, but today it rings hollow. It just too exactly duplicates the boy I knew decades ago when really I am curious about the man he might have become.

"I have to go," I say, using the age-old euphemism that always seems to serve.

He is the one caught off guard. He is the one saying how nice it was to hear my voice, perhaps hoping to keep me there longer.

But I am gone, refusing one more breath of these subtle but toxic fumes, the ones I used to inhale as deeply as the smoke from the ceramic pipe in the shape of a wizard.

LAST TIME

THE LAST TIME I SPOKE to my father was on Christmas Day. I called him. Maybe it took a few tries to get through. International circuits on Christmas Day get easily clogged.

Calling on Christmas Day was something I learned from him. That's what he used to do when I was little, calling back home to Budapest where the others still lived. Back then, he made an event out of calling so that somehow I always knew when he was making his Christmas Day call.

And now I was doing the same. Not making a huge deal of it, but calling on Christmas Day, calling back to Budapest, back to the same apartment on Böszörményi Út where my father had been calling decades ago.

I was calling from my home in Woodstock that my father had never seen. I had been reviewing our years together, chewing them over, not liking them, not liking them at all, and had seen no reason to continue a contact that was no contact.

Except today, on Christmas Day when I wanted just to please him, when I knew how easy it would be to do that. Just for him to hear my voice. It was one of the things I knew.

My aunt answered. Her English is minimal and so we can't say much except Merry Christmas and how are you and fine, fine – putting all our love into the inflection of our voices rather than any actual vocabulary.

And then she passes the phone to my father. "Beszélj angolul," she reminds him. "Speak English."

It's been over 20 years since his return to Hungary. He's in his 80s now. His signature has become a crooked spider, his notes to me typed by others.

My father takes the phone but does not speak. "Merry Christmas,

Dad!" I say with cheer and vigor. This is the part we have always been so good at: the cheerful beginning, like striking out on ice with a long bold stride and the undamaged hope that this time the ice will hold up and not crack and splinter underfoot.

Still he says nothing. I think I hear some kind of struggle as if the words are trapped in his throat and can't get out.

"Merry Christmas, Dad! How are you?" I wait for the response that always comes, the one that meets me at that pitch of connection before the undertow sets in.

But still he doesn't answer. There is just this almost silent struggle on the other end of the line.

I pause and wait. I don't know what to do. Perhaps I say something like, "Well, Dad, I hope you and Márta Néni have a good day together," to fill the silence a little and give him more time.

And then one strangled phrase makes it through. I can tell it is only a fragment of something longer that he wants to say. Torn from his throat, he gasps, "Keep in touch." It's a phrase I have heard him say a thousand times under a thousand circumstances. And here they are again, so familiar in his voice that they are beautiful. Keep in touch.

"Yes, Dad," I say. "I will." And it doesn't seem like we can do much more.

I think the dead are still present. I don't know for sure, but I think they are. That we can continue the conversation.

It is a riddle, a puzzle, this figure who took up so much space during most of my life, yet someone for whom I have not shed a tear. Not at all.

And yet I don't forget him. Maybe that is enough of a gift I can give him. Because I've had plenty of anger and disappointment to leave at his door, but it costs me nothing to remember him.

And he is someone who so wanted to be remembered. By the whole world. As a great statesman, or a great writer, or a great thinker. The dream that did not come true.

He did not think he could just exist. That was never ever enough. You had to do much more than just that if you wanted to be worth something.

But I don't need anything fancy like brilliance or fame or leatherbound books with his name on them to remember him. He lingers no matter what while I continue to question and examine and wind his Longines watch in the morning. Well, some mornings.

CPSIA information can be obtained
at www.ICGtesting.com
Printed in the USA
LVHW071448301222
736209LV00011B/395